The Psalms
for Prayer

Christmas 2003

Marge,

Since we have been prayer partners this past year, I thought this book using 'The Psalms' for prayer would help us in our prayer life.

This past year I'm sure has been your most difficult, yet your strength and courage has been an inspiration to many.

I Praise God for you!

God Bless You,
Joan Haas

The Psalms
for Prayer

T. M. Moore

Baker Books

A Division of Baker Book House Co
Grand Rapids, Michigan 49516

KJV
N E W
K I N G
J A M E S
VERSION®

Published by Baker Books
a division of Baker Book House Company
P.O. Box 6287, Grand Rapids, MI 49516-6287

Printed in the United States of America

Library of Congress Cataloging-in-Publication Data

Moore, T. M. (Terry Michael), 1949–
    The Psalms for prayer / T. M. Moore.
        p.   cm.
    Includes bibliographical references.
    ISBN 0-8010-6413-9 (pbk.)
    1. Bible. O. T. Psalms—Devotional use. 2. Prayer—Biblical
teaching. I. Title.
BS1430.4 .M58 2002
264′ .15—dc21   2002009126

For current information about all releases from Baker Book House, visit our web
site:
                    http://www.bakerbooks.com

Contents

Introduction

[The man who prays the psalms] will make the thoughts
of the psalms his own. He will sing them no longer as
verses composed by a prophet, but as born of his own
prayers. At least he should use them as intended for his
own mouth, and know that they were not fulfilled tem-
porarily in the prophet's age and circumstances, but are
being fulfilled in his daily life. [1]

Abba Isaac

Christians in every age have struggled with the discipline
of prayer. The many books, manuals, and seminars available today to teach and aid us in praying bear witness to
the fact that our generation is not immune to this chal-
lenge. In prayer, perhaps more than in any other of the
spiritual disciplines, we encounter distractions, diversions,
and all manner of difficulties which can keep us from
knowing the glory, joy, and power that a disciplined and
wholesome life of prayer can provide. Undoubtedly it is
not necessary to elaborate on these, for we have all expe-
rienced them: the wandering mind, a failure of words,
weariness of body or soul, the pressures of time, spiritual
oppression, and a certain inherent indisposition to prayer,
which may be a sign of unbelief as much as anything else.

We must admit that we do not know how to pray as
we should (Rom. 8:26) and that, therefore, we need all
the help we can get. But our gracious God is not indif-

ferent to our struggle; besides giving us His Spirit to aid in our prayers, He has provided a manual and guide to prayer that Christians in every age have found to be of invaluable assistance. Today many believers are once again beginning to discover the immensely satisfying and richly rewarding experience of coming to God in prayer through the vehicle of the psalms.[2]

The Book of Psalms is a rich treasury of prayers, confessions of faith, songs of praise and thanksgiving, memorials to God's grace and mercy, and celebrations of His faithfulness, goodness, and power. The psalms are of various types. *Wisdom psalms* show us the way of righteousness by contrasting it with wickedness and sin. *Royal psalms* celebrate, describe, or invoke the rule of the king or God Himself and help us to understand the order and character of His kingdom. *Psalms of complaint* show us the psalmist seeking God's help against some foe, or in the midst of some trial. *Psalms of praise* exalt God for His many virtues and lead the reader to praise Him in specific ways. *Psalms of thanksgiving* lead us in declaring our gratitude to God for His many blessings. *Testimony psalms* guide us in declaring our confidence in Him and exhort us to fulfill our vows. *Psalms of confession* help us in dealing with temptation and sin. *Psalms of admonition* warn of the judgment of God that is to come. And *psalms of imprecation* call down the wrath of God against the enemies of His people. By learning to use the psalms as a basis for our prayers we can realize greater consistency, delight, comprehensiveness, power, and satisfaction in this most foundational spiritual discipline. This edition of the Book of Psalms in the New King James Version is designed to guide you in making "God's prayer list" a more meaningful and valuable part of your own prayers.

In the following pages I want to introduce you to the discipline of praying the psalms. We will look first at the goal of praying the psalms. Then we will examine six ways of praying the psalms that can help us gain the most benefit from these 150 guides to prayer. As we shall see, these are not so much individual ways of praying as they are aspects of a single, overall approach to using the psalms in prayer. In addition, we will examine some difficulties that you can expect to encounter, and I will suggest ways of surmounting these in order to gain the most benefit from the discipline of praying the psalms. The rest of this brief introduction will explain the other aspects of this special edition of the Book of Psalms and how it can help you in making the psalms the basis and a growing staple of your own prayers.

The Goal of Praying the Psalms

Before we discuss the different ways of praying the psalms, let's make sure we understand the overall goal of this undertaking. I don't think I could say it any better than Abba Isaac did in the quote opening this introduction, or Athanasius did in the fourth century:

> He who recites the Psalms is uttering [them] as his own words, and each sings them as if they were written concerning him. . . . [H]e handles them as if he is speaking about himself. And the things spoken are such that he lifts them up to God as himself acting and speaking them from himself.[3]

The goal of learning to pray the psalms is *to allow the psalms to become your own prayers.* I'm not interested in promoting just another tedious devotional activity designed to enhance our sense of self-righteousness and enroll us in the ranks of modern Pharisees. Our purpose in praying the psalms is to be able to appropriate the words of the psalms as though they were our own words, to know and use these Spirit-given prayers, songs, and testimonies as our own prayers, and to be carried along by them in the power of God's Spirit as we come into the very presence of God.

Praying the psalms *can* become just like any other failed approach to prayer that you have ever tried. But it doesn't have to. If you can learn to make the psalms your own, to enter into the words of these songs, hymns, prayers, and confessions of faith as though they were your own words in prayer before the Lord, you will be able to find the power and satisfaction in prayer that we all earnestly desire. Like any worthwhile goal, achieving this one will take time and concentrated effort. With some psalms, you will find you can easily attain this objective. Others will take longer, while, if your experience is anything like my own, with some psalms you may struggle to achieve this goal for many, many years.

Two secondary goals derive from this main goal. First, I want to encourage you to begin praying the psalms as a regular discipline. That's not to say that the psalms are the only thing you will pray, or that whenever you pray you must find some psalm to use. Not at all. However, I do wish to encourage you to establish the practice of praying through the entire Psalter on a regular, disciplined basis, so that you become increasingly familiar with *all* the psalms. Thus you will gain the benefit in prayer that each of them has to offer.

Second, our goal is to have the psalms increasingly available to us whenever we pray, so that our prayers at the dinner table, with our families, in Bible studies, as we're driving in our cars—whenever—are informed and guided by the words and thoughts that are recorded in the psalms. The psalms came easily into the prayers of such biblical giants as David, Solomon, Jonah, Daniel, and the apostles. One reason we find their prayers peppered with quotes from and allusions to the psalms may be that they had become familiar with these through regular, disciplined praying through the Psalter. The practice of great saints throughout the history of the church also reflects this facility with using the psalms in prayer, undoubtedly for the same reason. Learning to integrate Scripture into all our prayers can only serve to strengthen our prayers, to give us more confidence in prayer, and to provide us with words to use in coming before God's throne of grace as often as we have opportunity or need. You will find that this goal begins to be unconsciously achieved as you work at praying the psalms in a regular, disciplined way.

I think we can agree that these are worthy goals. To be able to pray more consistently, more powerfully, and more confidently is surely a desire of every sincere Christian. Praying the psalms—making them your own prayers in your own words—can help you to reach that objective.

Praying the Psalms

The six ways of praying the psalms that I will discuss should be looked at like spokes on a wheel. In order for the wheel to do its work, all the spokes have to be in place and functioning properly. As the wheel turns, only the spoke that is perpendicular to the ground is required to bear the weight of the load at any given time; however, because the wheel is in constant motion, all the spokes must be strong and functioning, ready to serve as needed.

In the same way, the methods of praying the psalms that we will consider in this introduction are not intended for use with any particular psalm or any particular type of psalm. Rather, we will use all of them together during the course of our prayers (indeed, this is the last of the six "spokes" which I will describe). The methods I will be presenting have this much in common: they are all ways of allowing the psalms to guide, inform, and carry our prayers before the Lord. The differences between them are not dramatic; as I have said, these are not so much distinct approaches to praying the psalms as aspects of one overall approach to using God's prayer list.

The objective is to be able to move from one method to another as we work our way through a psalm, so that, ultimately, we should almost become unaware of using any specific method of praying for any particular psalm, or any portion of any psalm, and be able to pray as the Lord leads us, mastering all the methods of praying the psalms and employing them freely and easily all together.

Let's look, then, at six ways of praying the psalms that can help you begin to find greater power and satisfaction in your prayers.

Verbatim Praying

Some of the psalms lend themselves to what I call *verbatim praying*. That is, we can simply pray the words that are right there in the text, without any need to change, adapt, or interpret them. The psalm says exactly what we want to say, and we can pray effectively using the words just as they are. We may feel free to add our own words, following those of the psalmist, or to allow the psalm to lead us into related subjects for prayer, but, for the most part, we find the words of the psalm perfectly adequate for the purposes of our prayer.

While this way of praying the psalms is best suited for portions of many psalms, it can be employed with entire psalms as well. For example, take a few moments right now and pray through Psalm 65, using only the words that are given in the text:

Praise is awaiting You, O God, in Zion;
And to You the vow shall be performed.
O You who hear prayer,
To You all flesh will come.
Iniquities prevail against me;
As for our transgressions,
You will provide atonement for them.

Blessed *is the man whom* You choose,
And cause to approach *You,*
That he may dwell in Your courts.
We shall be satisfied with the goodness of Your
    house,
Of Your holy temple.

By awesome deeds in righteousness You will answer
    us,
O God of our salvation,
You who are the confidence of all the ends of the
    earth,
And of the far-off seas;
Who established the mountains by His strength,
Being clothed with power;
You who still the noise of the seas,
The noise of their waves,
And the tumult of the peoples.
They also who dwell in the farthest parts are afraid of
    Your signs;

13

> You make the outgoings of the morning and evening
>   rejoice.
>
> You visit the earth and water it;
> You greatly enrich it;
> The river of God is full of water;
> You provide their grain,
> For so You have prepared it.
> You water its ridges abundantly,
> You settle its furrows;
> You make it soft with showers,
> You bless its growth.
>
> You crown the year with Your goodness,
> And Your paths drip *with* abundance.
> They drop *on* the pastures of the wilderness.
> And the little hills rejoice on every side.
> The pastures are clothed with flocks;
> The valleys also are covered with grain;
> They shout for joy, they also sing.

Psalm 65 is a psalm of praise to God. I ask you to consider: how much richer, more glorious, and more satisfying is praying this psalm verbatim than simply praying, "Lord, we really just praise You"? Many psalms, and many more portions of psalms, can easily be appropriated in prayer through simple verbatim praying.

Other psalms that lend themselves to this method may require a little more reflection as we are praying. They may include unfamiliar allusions, historical referents, or doctrinal difficulties, encouraging us to slow down and listen to the Lord more carefully as we pray. We may need to pause to reflect, to let the Spirit illuminate God's Word, to consider how we might express the thoughts of the psalm in our own words, or to pray for specific individuals or needs that come to mind by the prompting of the Holy Spirit. And we may do all this in the context of simply praying the straightforward words of the text itself.

Praying any psalm verbatim requires that we have a good feel for what the psalm is about. Learning the message of each psalm will come over time, with repeated use, study, and meditation. Verbatim praying is the easiest way to begin using the psalms as God's prayer list for our lives. As I mentioned, this method can be adapted to praying parts of almost all the psalms. Other entire psalms that lend themselves to this method are Psalms 8, 38, 44, 51, 56, 57, 67, and 80. These provide a good place to start in learning how to use the psalms in prayer, for they require nothing more of us than to pray the very words God Himself has provided, reflecting on their meaning and significance as we proceed.

Paraphrase Praying

A second way to use God's prayer list is what I call *paraphrase praying.* Typically, when I am using this method, I will read over the section of the psalm that lends itself to paraphrasing, then go back and pray it according to how I think I can use it for my own life. This kind of praying is useful when the wording or circumstances of the psalm do not *exactly* fit our own, but bring to mind something very similar. For example, here is Psalm 59:1–4:

> Deliver me from my enemies, O my God;
> Defend me from those who rise up against me.
> Deliver me from the workers of iniquity,
> And save me from bloodthirsty men.
>
> For look, they lie in wait for my life;
> The mighty gather against me,

Not *for* my transgressions nor *for* my sin, O LORD.
They run and prepare themselves through no fault *of mine*.

Awake to help me, and behold!

Most of us do not have enemies like this lying in the bushes waiting to attack and destroy us. David did, however, and God gave him these words to use in seeking His protection against foes.

Yet we do have spiritual enemies constantly lying in wait to attack us and trip us up, as Paul reminds us (Eph. 6:12). And we do need the help and protection of the Lord in dealing with them—to recognize and resist the temptations they bring against us, to guard against falling into step with sinful lifestyles, and so on. Thus, having read these verses of Psalm 59 in a prayerful mode, we might rephrase, or *paraphrase,* them as follows:

Lord, deliver me from those spiritual forces of wickedness in high places that seek to distract and destroy me every day. Keep my focus on high, on You and on my Lord Jesus. Help me to recognize the temptations that come against me every day; do not let me be overly influenced by the sinful ways of others; help me to be on my guard against the devil, who I know is stalking about like a roaring lion, today as ever. Lord, rise to my defense as I seek to stand strong in the battle that is before me today, and keep me strong through every temptation and trial.

In paraphrase praying, it is best to first read through the part of the psalm you are going to pray, usually a stanza or so (conveniently divided for us in the New King James Version). Then spend a few moments meditating on the meaning of the verses you have read, especially how they might touch on some situation or need in your own life or that of someone you know. Then, as you read back through the verses again, put them into words more appropriate to your own situation, letting the Spirit guide you by His inspired words as you bring your particular need or request before the Lord, using the prompting provided by each verse. In my experience, this kind of praying can be useful in working through many of the psalms, as well as portions of most of them. You might try Psalms 9, 26, 36, 62, and 84 as good places to start in practicing the method of paraphrase praying. In due time you will find that you can pray even as you are first reading a psalm before the Lord in prayer.

Praying Over a Psalm

Somewhat similar to paraphrase praying—and probably deriving from it as a result of constant use—is what I call *praying over a psalm.* I have found this method especially useful for those psalms which recount God's saving work for Israel or His sovereignty over the world (such as Psalms 78 and 104). In this method, being very familiar with the content of the psalm and the flow of its argument, I will simply summarize large sections and try to apply them to my own circumstances as I read, praying as I scan through the psalm. My prayer may not include every verse of the psalm; rather, I'm trying to capture the thrust of a stanza and make it my own.

For example, Psalm 104 surveys the sovereign grace of God in providing for His creation. It begins with a declaration of His eternal majesty and splendor (vv. 1–2), then moves to a proclamation of His work as Creator and Lord (vv. 3–4). From there the psalm surveys God's providential sustenance of all He has made (vv.

5–30), ending with a paean of praise and a commitment to perpetual praise and rejoicing (vv. 31–35).

As I read through this psalm I simply summarize in prayer the content or theme of each stanza, letting my prayer be guided by the psalm, but allowing it to go in whatever direction I may be inclined. For example, here is how I might pray over vv. 18–23 (you might want to keep an eye on these verses in your own Bible as you read my prayer):

> Lord, You have provided shelter for every one of Your creatures, including me. I thank You that, as You have given the mountains for wild goats, the hills for the rock badger, and places for every other creature, You have given me this home, with all its furnishings and blessings. I thank You for the different seasons of the year and the beauty each affords; for the day and the night, time to work and time to rest; and for a proper place for everything in my life. Thank You for the work You've given me to do. Here are the tasks I'm facing today. . . . Help me to be faithful in them, even as Your other creatures faithfully pursue the work You've called them to each day.

The main difference between this way of praying and paraphrase praying is that, having become very familiar with the content of the psalm, I allow the *themes* in a stanza of the psalm to prompt me to pray according to the subject they suggest, and am not so wedded to the actual *words* of individual verses, as I am inclined to be in paraphrase praying. Often, as I am praying over a psalm, my prayers will branch out into many related subject areas as the Spirit prompts my mind and takes my prayers in new and exciting directions through the psalm.

Here is another example of this way of praying from Psalm 106:6–12 (again, have a look at these verses as you read my prayer):

> Lord, we are sinners just like our fathers in the wilderness were. We are as wicked and evil as they were. Just as they so easily lost sight of all You did for them, so do we, so do I. Just as they forgot all your kindness toward them, so do we, so do I. We have become complacent about our mission; we have kept idols; we have compromised morally in many ways. Like them, we are deserving of your judgment. Yet You saved them; You continued to support them; You showed Your grace to them in spite of the hardness of their hearts. You delivered them from all their enemies; You moved heaven and earth to deliver them to Yourself. They believed You then, and they sang Your praise. I praise You, too, Lord, for the way You delivered me from my sin and made me Your own dear child. Help me to remember Your kindness to me, and let me never lose sight of all You have done for me. (Here I might rehearse some recent examples of His kindness.)

I find it useful, from time to time, to carefully read through the psalms that I typically pray over so I don't miss anything due to familiarity. About every third or fourth time I come to one of these psalms, I will read it through a stanza at a time, meditating and reflecting carefully on each verse, then go back and pray over it as usual, or paraphrase pray it, incorporating any new themes or insights I might have gained.

Responsive Praying

A fourth method for praying the psalms is what I call *responsive praying.* Here the psalm presents a theme, an idea, or a situation, although the psalm is not itself in the form of a prayer. I read through the psalm a verse or a stanza at a time, then pray it back to the Lord, responding as the psalm guides me. I consider that God is speaking to me in the psalm, and I am responding to a subject of interest to Him.

Here, for example, is how I might pray Psalm 1 responsively, with the psalm and my prayer alternating:

Blessed *is* the man
> Who walks not in the counsel of the ungodly,
> Nor stands in the path of sinners,
> Nor sits in the seat of the scornful;
But his delight *is* in the law of the Lord,
> And in His law he meditates day and night.

Lord, I seek Your blessings for this day. Keep me from sin. Do not let me listen to sinful counsel. Keep my feet in the way of righteousness, and do not let me "settle in" to any sinful ways. Lord, help me to delight in Your law, to read and study it with joy and care, to think about Your Word throughout the day, and to consider carefully its meaning for my life.

He shall be like a tree
> Planted by the rivers of water,
> That brings forth its fruit in its season,
> Whose leaf also shall not wither;
And whatever he does shall prosper.

Root me deeply in Your Word, O Lord, and let the river of Your grace water me afresh every day! Bring forth the fruit of righteousness in me, the fruit of the Spirit and the tokens of love, the fruit of powerful witness to You, and the fruit of holy living. You know the things I'm struggling with. . . . Let me prosper in all that I seek to do for You, O Lord, including those responsibilities and opportunities that are before me today. (Here I might name some things on my daily schedule or some people I am seeking to witness to.)

The ungodly *are* not so,
But *are* like the chaff which the wind drives away.
Therefore the ungodly shall not stand in the
    judgment,
Nor sinners in the congregation of the righteous.

Lord, this morning I think of those people I know who do not know You. I'm reminded of . . . (Here I name the people in my personal mission field for whom I regularly pray and with whom I seek opportunities for witness. If they have particular needs, I bring those to the Lord at this time. I also pray for an opportunity to talk with one or more of them, especially those who I might see this day.) Lord, give them a sense of their responsibility to You. Make them mindful of Your judgment. Help them to seek You, so that they might become part of Your family as well.

For the LORD knows the way of the righteous,
But the way of the ungodly shall perish.

Lord, I know that You look on me as righteous only because of what Jesus has done for me. You have clothed me in His righteousness, and You are working out Your salvation in righteousness in me. I know that You will watch over my way today, and I thank You for delivering me from eternal wrath. Let those who do not know You see something of Jesus in me today, O Lord, and let that be a spark to turn them from wickedness to You.

Responsive praying thus establishes a dialogue with God in which, as He speaks from His Word, we can respond in a manner appropriate to our circumstances or needs. For this reason I find this to be one of the richest methods of praying the psalms. Many psalms lend themselves to this kind of praying, such as Psalms 37, 73, 87, 99, and 114.

Guided Praying

Another way to pray the psalms is what I call *guided praying.* In fact, you can use this method with any of the other methods mentioned thus far. The distinctive of this method is that the psalm is actually guiding you to pray for something particularly pressing in your life or the life of someone else. The psalm presents a theme so clearly parallel to your own circumstances, or those of someone you know, that you let the verses suggest a topic, and then you continue in prayer for as many specific applications of that topic as the Lord is pleased to bring to your mind.

For example, Psalm 67 clearly lends itself to praying for missions. Here you can let the Spirit guide you to pray about missions organizations, missionaries, your church's missions program, or your own involvement in missions. Think about the specific ways God has blessed you and your church, and ask Him to help you be good stewards of those blessings for the purpose of helping others know Him.

Psalm 129 deals with persecution. You can use it to pray for believers who are being persecuted for their faith, naming specific countries, situations, or people as the Lord brings them to mind, or praising the Lord for the faithfulness of those who have suffered in the past.

Psalm 47 envisions the Lord ruling over all the nations, and the princes of the nations becoming the people of the God of Abraham. This psalm leads me to think of the church's work in evangelism, calling the nations to believe the gospel and submit to King Jesus. I pray for my own evangelism in my personal mission field, for the evangelistic outreach of our church, and for churches in my community and around the world. In the margin next to this psalm I have penciled in the names of churches where I have led seminars in evangelism, and I am reminded to pray that they will be faithful in what they have learned. This psalm leads me to pray that God would rekindle the fire of evangelism in His people, that He would begin to work in the hearts of unbelievers and prepare them to hear the gospel, and that He would bring a mighty harvest into His house.

Psalm 72 leads in praying for our government officials. Psalm 80 seeks revival in the church. Psalm 73 deals with temptation. If our minds are engaged as we are praying the psalms, we will find that they guide us to think of many specific needs, people, or situations in our lives and the lives of those we know and love. We may pencil some of these in the margin, or use Post-it notes, to remind ourselves to pray for them. The Spirit can prompt us, bringing to mind the kinds of things He wants us to pray for on any given day, but we must be willing to be guided and to let the psalms do their work of suggesting items for prayer before the throne of grace.

Combination Praying

The final method of praying the psalms is really a combination of all of the previous methods. As you begin to master the various ways of praying the psalms, you will find that you can move easily from one method to another as you work your way through any particular psalm. This is characteristically how I pray the psalms, as I allow the form, content, or theme of a psalm to suggest the best way of praying it. For example, I may begin praying Psalm 18 verbatim (vv. 1–3), then move through paraphrase praying (vv. 4–15), praying over the psalm (vv. 16–24), verbatim praying again (vv. 25–29), responsive praying (vv. 30–45), and then verbatim praying once again to wrap it up (vv. 46–50). I'm usually not conscious of making these switches. Because I am familiar with how to use each method and I carefully follow the form or content of the psalm, I can move back and forth with relative ease in a fairly smooth and richly rewarding prayer.

Some Other Suggestions

In addition to these methods of praying the psalms, you will need a few other helps to guide you. For example, in order to make the words of the psalms your own words you will often need to change the person or number indicated in the psalm—from third person, say, to second, or from singular to plural (or vice versa). In our prayers we want to talk *to* the Lord, and not merely *about* Him, and we want to use His words in the way most relevant for our own situations.

Many allusions and references to Israel will be found in the Book of Psalms. What shall we do with these? The New Testament teaches us to think of the church and her situation as the new Israel (Heb. 12:22–24). Thus, references to the temple can lead us to think of our own church; the land of promise suggests all the promises God has given us in Jesus; Israel's enemies recall our spiritual adversaries, as well as those who persecute the church; and Israel's judges and kings can call to mind the leaders of our church and nation.

A psalm may not exactly fit your circumstances. Pray it for someone else. Even if you're not suffering like the narrator of Psalm 88, some people are, and you can pray for them even if you don't know their names. Or pray that God would prepare you for such situations in your own life. For example, as you pray Psalm 42 or 43, you may not feel discouraged or troubled, but you can ask God to give you strength to hope in Him and praise Him when you do experience trials. Or you may be praying through Psalm 119 and find that its many declarations of love for and trust in God's Word don't quite describe you. You can make what the Hebrew language calls a *jussive* out of these psalms: "Lord, *let* Your Word abide in me," "Help me to love Your law," "*Let* me meditate more frequently and deeply on Your Word," and so forth. As the psalm guides you and you reflect on its words, make the words your own by such simple and relevant adaptations as these.

What shall we do with psalms of imprecation, such as Psalm 137? In these the psalmist angrily calls down the wrath of God against the enemies of His people, often using quite violent imagery. Keeping in mind the request in Psalm 83:16 that God's pressure on our foes might bring them to shame and repentance, I believe we can still pray these psalms with confidence without compromising the Lord's requirement that we pray for and love our enemies (Matt. 6:43–48). True believers have many adversaries, not the least of whom is the enemy of our souls and his spiritual henchmen. Surely we can pray that God would thwart our enemies, convict them, and even, should they insist on persisting in their torment, bring them to naught.

Finally, look for Christ in each psalm. Remember that He is interceding for you at the Father's right hand (Heb. 7:25; 1 John 2:1). Recall His saving work, His righteousness, and His imminent return in judgment. Claim His righteousness as your own. Exalt Him as King and Lord. Call upon Him in your times of need. Each one of the psalms can lead us to think about Jesus in deeper and more personal ways as we use these guides to prayer from the perspective of knowing Him.

How to Use This Edition of the Psalms

This edition of the Book of Psalms in the New King James Version is specifically prepared for use as a manual and guide to prayer. Each psalm is preceded by a brief introduction explaining the psalm's type, its content or argument, and the place of Christ in the psalm.[4] In addition, a New Testament reference has been included to guide you in thinking more clearly about how to use each psalm in prayer. This will help you get a feel for the theme of the psalm and may suggest some subjects for prayer. Each psalm is divided by headings, which are intended to prompt your prayers. Follow the suggestions of the headings as you read and pray through the psalm, and you'll find it easier to make the words of the psalm your own.

As you get started praying the psalms, I suggest you find several that you can pray verbatim. Begin to do this right away. Then, using those same psalms, start to practice all the other methods I have described. From there you should be able to branch out to any of the psalms with relative ease.

Alternatively, you might take some psalms that you already know well and love. This is how I began praying the psalms. Psalms 8, 19, and 23, besides being wonderful prayers, were my own training ground in beginning to pray the psalms. I had studied them, found that I returned to them often in my life and teaching, and loved them enough to have memorized each of them.

As you gain confidence and ease in using the psalms as God's prayer list, you will want to work toward praying through the entire Psalter on a regular basis. This book concludes with three schedules for your use: one for praying through the psalms in seven weeks, one for praying through them in one month, and one for praying through them in one week (a little ambitious for most, but useful for a time of spiritual retreat). Each of these schedules is broken down into different times for prayer each day. This biblical practice of setting aside particular times during the day for prayer has been emulated by Christians throughout the ages who have sought to redeem some of their mundane time for kingdom business.

The key is to start right away to let God's prayer list begin to have a more prominent role in your own prayers. Yes, it may be awkward at first, even difficult, and you may need to make some changes in your prayer life. But you can begin praying the psalms today, right now, and with ever increasing power, satisfaction, and joy as God's prayer list becomes your prayer list as well.

I would like to thank Nelson Keener at Baker Books for his faithful support of this project, as well as my wife, Susie, for her many excellent suggestions and careful proofreading of the original draft. My prayer is that readers will find this discipline as rich and rewarding as I have over the years. May God be pleased to increase the chorus of us who come with ever increasing frequency before His throne of grace, using His own words to find help in their time of need, lavishing Him with praise and thanks as we do.

The Psalms
for Prayer

Psalm 1

This wisdom psalm sets forth the righteousness for which the believer is to strive, but which we can only fully realize in the righteousness of Christ. Read Philippians 3:7–11.

Seek grace for sanctification.

¹Blessed *is* the man
    Who walks not in the counsel of the ungodly,
    Nor stands in the path of sinners,
    Nor sits in the seat of the scornful;
²But his delight *is* in the law of the LORD,
    And in His law he meditates day and night.
³He shall be like a tree
    Planted by the rivers of water,
    That brings forth its fruit in its season,
    Whose leaf also shall not wither;
And whatever he does shall prosper.

Intercede for the lost.

⁴The ungodly *are* not so,
But *are* like the chaff which the wind drives away.
⁵Therefore the ungodly shall not stand in the
    judgment,
Nor sinners in the congregation of the righteous.

Praise the Lord for His sovereignty in salvation.

⁶For the LORD knows the way of the righteous,
But the way of the ungodly shall perish.

Psalm 2

A royal psalm celebrating the enthronement of God's king and of Christ and calling the nations to submit to Him. Read Acts 2:36; Philippians 2:5–11.

Review the world's rebellion against the Lord.

¹Why do the nations rage,
And the people plot a vain thing?
²The kings of the earth set themselves,
And the rulers take counsel together,
Against the LORD and against His Anointed, *saying,*
³"Let us break Their bonds in pieces
And cast away Their cords from us."

Praise God for His exalted King.

⁴He who sits in the heavens shall laugh;
The Lord shall hold them in derision.
⁵Then He shall speak to them in His wrath,
And distress them in His deep displeasure:
⁶"Yet I have set My King
On My holy hill of Zion."

Praise God for His promise that Christ should inherit the nations.

⁷"I will declare the decree:
The LORD has said to Me,
'You *are* My Son,
Today I have begotten You.
⁸Ask of Me, and I will give *You*
The nations *for* Your inheritance,
And the ends of the earth *for* Your possession.
⁹You shall break them with a rod of iron;
You shall dash them in pieces like a potter's vessel.'"

Pray for the nations to heed the call of the gospel.

> [10]Now therefore, be wise, O kings;
> Be instructed, you judges of the earth.
> [11]Serve the LORD with fear,
> And rejoice with trembling.

Pray that they and we may be vibrant in our love for Christ.

> [12]Kiss the Son, lest He be angry,
> And you perish *in* the way,
> When His wrath is kindled but a little.
> Blessed *are* all those who put their trust in Him.

Psalm 3

David's psalm of complaint reminds us of the spiritual war-
fare in which we are daily engaged, and in which we rest in
the victory of Christ. Read Ephesians 6:10–20; Romans 8:37.

A Psalm of David when he fled from Absalom his son.

Recall the enemies of God, human and spiritual.

> [1]LORD, how they have increased who trouble me!
> Many *are* they who rise up against me.
> [2]Many *are* they who say of me,
> "*There* is no help for him in God."

Selah

Declare your confidence in God's help.

> [3]But You, O LORD, *are* a shield for me,
> My glory and the One who lifts up my head.

⁴I cried to the LORD with my voice,
And He heard me from His holy hill.

Selah

⁵I lay down and slept;
I awoke, for the LORD sustained me.
⁶I will not be afraid of ten thousands of people
Who have set *themselves* against me all around.

**Call upon the Lord, who defeats all our enemies,
for deliverance.**

⁷Arise, O LORD;
Save me, O my God!
For You have struck all my enemies on the
        cheekbone;
You have broken the teeth of the ungodly.

Praise the Lord for His saving mercy.

⁸Salvation *belongs* to the LORD.
Your blessing *is* upon Your people.

Selah

Psalm 4

*David confidently testifies of his trust in the Lord in the face
of unknown adversity and leads us to express our trust in
Christ during our own trials. Read Romans 8:35–39.*

To the Chief Musician. With stringed instruments. A Psalm of David.

Seek the mercy of God in the face of adversity.

¹Hear me when I call,
O God of my righteousness!

You have relieved me *when I was* in distress;
Have mercy on me, and hear my prayer.

²How long, O you sons of men,
Will you turn my glory to shame?
How long will you love worthlessness
And seek falsehood?

Selah

³But know that the Lord has set apart for Himself
  him who is godly;
The Lord will hear when I call to Him.

Meditate on God's goodness, give thanks, and seek the Lord's peace.

⁴Be angry, and do not sin.
Meditate within your heart on your bed, and be still.

Selah

⁵Offer the sacrifices of righteousness,
And put your trust in the Lord.

Seek the renewing grace of God, and rest in Him.

⁶*There are* many who say,
"Who will show us *any* good?"
Lord, lift up the light of Your countenance upon us.
⁷You have put gladness in my heart,
More than in the season that their grain and wine
  increased.
⁸I will both lie down in peace, and sleep;
For You alone, O Lord, make me dwell in safety.

Psalm 5

This wisdom psalm counsels us to resist temptation and to seek the Lord for the righteousness of Christ that is pleasing to Him. Read 1 Corinthians 10:13–14.

To the Chief Musician. With flutes. A Psalm of David.

Cry to God to hear your prayer.

¹Give ear to my words, O LORD,
Consider my meditation.
²Give heed to the voice of my cry,
My King and my God,
For to You I will pray.
³My voice You shall hear in the morning, O LORD;
In the morning I will direct *it* to You,
And I will look up.

Seek God's help in resisting temptation.

⁴For You *are* not a God who takes pleasure in
    wickedness,
Nor shall evil dwell with You.
⁵The boastful shall not stand in Your sight;
You hate all workers of iniquity.
⁶You shall destroy those who speak falsehood;
The LORD abhors the bloodthirsty and deceitful man.

Thank God for His mercy, worship Him, and seek His righteousness.

⁷But as for me, I will come into Your house in the
    multitude of Your mercy;
In fear of You I will worship toward Your holy
    temple.
⁸Lead me, O LORD, in Your righteousness because of
    my enemies;
Make Your way straight before my face.

Rest in God's justice toward the wicked.

9For *there is* no faithfulness in their mouth;
Their inward part *is* destruction;
Their throat *is* an open tomb;
They flatter with their tongue.
10Pronounce them guilty, O God!
Let them fall by their own counsels;
Cast them out in the multitude of their
    transgressions,
For they have rebelled against You.

Rejoice and praise God for His saving protection.

11But let all those rejoice who put their trust in You;
Let them ever shout for joy, because You defend
    them;
Let those also who love Your name
Be joyful in You.
12For You, O LORD, will bless the righteous;
With favor You will surround him as *with* a shield.

Psalm 6

In this psalm of complaint David teaches us to cry out to the Lord in the midst of every adversity, that we may obtain mercy and find grace to help in our time of need. Read Hebrews 4:16.

To the Chief Musician. With stringed instruments. On an eight-stringed harp. A Psalm of David.

Seek mercy in times of trouble.

1O LORD, do not rebuke me in Your anger,
Nor chasten me in Your hot displeasure.

²Have mercy on me, O LORD, for I *am* weak;
O LORD, heal me, for my bones are troubled;
³My soul also is greatly troubled;
But You, O LORD—how long?

⁴Return, O LORD, deliver me!
Oh, save me for Your mercies' sake!
⁵For in death *there is* no remembrance of You;
In the grave who will give You thanks?

Express your trouble to the Lord.

⁶I am weary with my groaning;
All night I make my bed swim;
I drench my couch with my tears.
⁷My eye wastes away because of grief;
It grows old because of all my enemies.

Rest in the Lord's grace and victory.

⁸Depart from me, all you workers of iniquity;
For the LORD has heard the voice of my weeping.
⁹The LORD has heard my supplication;
The LORD will receive my prayer.
¹⁰Let all my enemies be ashamed and greatly
    troubled;
Let them turn back *and* be ashamed suddenly.

Psalm 7

In this psalm of testimony David confidently asserts his trust in the Lord and His righteous judgment. Read Romans 8:1–4, 31.

A Meditation of David, which he sang to the LORD concerning the words of Cush, a Benjamite.

Seek God's help against foes.

¹O LORD my God, in You I put my trust;
Save me from all those who persecute me;
And deliver me,
²Lest they tear me like a lion,
Rending *me* in pieces, while *there is* none to deliver.

Let God search you for any lingering sin.

³O LORD my God, if I have done this:
If there is any iniquity in my hands,
⁴If I have repaid evil to him who was at peace with
     me,
Or have plundered my enemy without cause,
⁵Let the enemy pursue me and overtake *me;*
Yes, let him trample my life to the earth,
And lay my honor in the dust.

Selah

Call upon the Lord for deliverance.

⁶Arise, O LORD, in Your anger;
Lift Yourself up because of the rage of my enemies,
And awake for me *to* the judgment You have
     commanded!
⁷So the congregation of the peoples shall surround
     You;
For their sakes, therefore, return on high.

Express confidence in the Lord's righteous judgment.

⁸The LORD shall judge the peoples;
Judge me, O LORD, according to my righteousness,
And according to my integrity within me.

⁹Oh, let the wickedness of the wicked come to an
    end.
But establish the just;
For the righteous God tests the hearts and minds.
¹⁰My defense *is* of God,
Who saves the upright in heart.

¹¹God *is* a just judge,
And God is angry *with the wicked* every day.
¹²If he does not turn back,
He will sharpen His sword;
He bends His bow and makes it ready.
¹³He also prepares for Himself instruments of death;
He makes His arrows into fiery shafts.

Release the wicked to God's judgment, and praise His righteous name.

¹⁴Behold, *the wicked* travails with iniquity,
Conceives trouble and brings forth falsehood.
¹⁵He made a pit and dug it out,
And has fallen into the ditch *which* he made.
¹⁶His trouble shall return upon his own head,
And his violent dealing shall come down on his own
    crown.

¹⁷I will praise the LORD according to His
    righteousness,
And will sing praise to the name of the LORD Most
    High.

Psalm 8

Let this psalm of praise and wonder lead you to glorify God for the way He has revealed Himself in the things He has made and for your calling to serve Him in His kingdom. Read Romans 11:33–36.

To the Chief Musician. On the instrument of Gath. A Psalm of David.

Praise the excellence of God's name, revealed in creation.

¹O LORD, our Lord,
How excellent *is* Your name in all the earth,
You who set Your glory above the heavens!

²Out of the mouth of babes and infants
You have ordained strength,
Because of Your enemies,
That You may silence the enemy and the avenger.

Praise God for His grace in creating you and giving you dominion.

³When I consider Your heavens, the work of Your
fingers,
The moon and the stars, which You have ordained,
⁴What is man that You are mindful of him,
And the son of man that You visit him?
⁵For You have made him a little lower than the
angels.
And You have crowned him with glory and honor.

⁶You have made him to have dominion over the
works of Your hands;
You have put all *things* under his feet,
⁷All sheep and oxen—
Even the beasts of the field,

8The birds of the air,
And the fish of the sea
That pass through the paths of the seas.

Praise God's excellent name.

9O LORD, our Lord,
How excellent *is* Your name in all the earth!

Psalm 9

David praises the Lord and expresses confidence in His righteous judgment and saving mercy. Read 2 Timothy 1:12.

To the Chief Musician. To *the tune of* "Death of the Son." A Psalm of David.

Praise God for His greatness, and rejoice in Him.

1I will praise *You,* O LORD, with my whole heart;
I will tell of all Your marvelous works.
2I will be glad and rejoice in You;
I will sing praise to Your name, O Most High.

Thank God for, and express confidence in, His protection from enemies.

3When my enemies turn back,
They shall fall and perish at Your presence.
4For You have maintained my right and my cause;
You sat on the throne judging in righteousness.
5You have rebuked the nations,
You have destroyed the wicked;
You have blotted out their name forever and ever.

6O enemy, destructions are finished forever!
And you have destroyed cities;
Even their memory has perished.

⁷But the LORD shall endure forever;
He has prepared His throne for judgment.
⁸He shall judge the world in righteousness,
And He shall administer judgment for the peoples in
    uprightness.
⁹The LORD also will be a refuge for the oppressed,
A refuge in times of trouble.
¹⁰And those who know Your name will put their trust
    in You;
For You, LORD, have not forsaken those who seek
    You.

Praise the Lord and seek His mercy in the time of judgment.

¹¹Sing praises to the LORD, who dwells in Zion!
Declare His deeds among the people.
¹²When He avenges blood, He remembers them;
He does not forget the cry of the humble.

¹³Have mercy on me, O LORD!
Consider my trouble from those who hate me,
You who lift me up from the gates of death,
¹⁴That I may tell of all Your praise
In the gates of the daughter of Zion.
I will rejoice in Your salvation.

¹⁵The nations have sunk down in the pit *which* they
    made;
In the net which they hid, their own foot is caught.
¹⁶The LORD is known *by* the judgment He executes;
The wicked is snared in the work of his own hands.

                                    Meditation. Selah
¹⁷The wicked shall be turned into hell,
And all the nations that forget God.
¹⁸For the needy shall not always be forgotten;
The expectation of the poor shall *not* perish forever.

Call upon God for justice against the wicked.

¹⁹Arise, O LORD,
Do not let man prevail;
Let the nations be judged in Your sight.
²⁰Put them in fear, O LORD,
That the nations may know themselves *to be but* men.

Selah

Psalm 10

This is a psalm of imprecation, calling upon the Lord to rise up against His enemies and to comfort and rescue His afflicted ones. It is appropriate, keeping Psalm 83:16 in mind, to pray this against those who persecute the church, especially our spiritual foes. Read Revelation 12:9–11.

Recall the suffering of the persecuted church.

¹Why do You stand afar off, O LORD?
Why do You hide *Yourself* in times of trouble?
²The wicked in *his* pride persecutes the poor;
Let them be caught in the plots which they have
devised.
³For the wicked boasts of his heart's desire;
He blesses the greedy *and* renounces the LORD.
⁴The wicked in his proud countenance does not seek
God.
God *is* in none of his thoughts.

Deplore the arrogance of all God's foes.

⁵His ways are always prospering;
Your judgments *are* far above, out of his sight;

As for all his enemies, he sneers at them.
⁶He has said in his heart,
"I shall not be moved;
I shall never be in adversity."
⁷His mouth is full of cursing and deceit and
  oppression;
Under his tongue *is* trouble and iniquity.

Intercede for those who are persecuted by the wicked.

⁸He sits in the lurking places of the villages;
In the secret places he murders the innocent;
His eyes are secretly fixed on the helpless.
⁹He lies in wait secretly, as a lion in his den;
He lies in wait to catch the poor;
He catches the poor when he draws him into his net.
¹⁰So he crouches, he lies low,
That the helpless may fall by his strength.
¹¹He has said in his heart,
"God has forgotten;
He hides His face;
He will never see *it.*"

Cry to God to intervene against persecutors.

¹²Arise, O LORD!
O God, lift up Your hand!
Do not forget the humble.
¹³Why do the wicked renounce God?
He has said in his heart,
"You will not require *an account.*"
¹⁴But You have seen *it,* for You observe trouble and
  grief,
To repay *it* by Your hand.
The helpless commits himself to You;
You are the helper of the fatherless.
¹⁵Break the arm of the wicked and the evil *man;*
Seek out his wickedness *until* You find none.

Exalt the Lord for His sovereignty and justice.

¹⁶The LORD *is* King forever and ever;
The nations have perished out of His land.
¹⁷LORD, You have heard the desire of the humble;
You will prepare their heart;
You will cause Your ear to hear,
¹⁸To do justice to the fatherless and the oppressed,
That the man of the earth may oppress no more.

Psalm 11

Use this testimony psalm to express your confidence in our sovereign, loving Lord in the face of every adversity or trial. Read 1 Peter 4:12–19.

To the Chief Musician. *A Psalm* of David.

Trust in God, and resist the temptation to fear.

¹In the LORD I put my trust;
How can you say to my soul,
"Flee *as* a bird to your mountain"?
²For look! The wicked bend *their* bow,
They make ready their arrow on the string,
That they may shoot secretly at the upright in heart.
³If the foundations are destroyed,
What can the righteous do?

Rest in God's sovereign care.

⁴The LORD *is* in His holy temple,
The LORD's throne *is* in heaven;
His eyes behold,
His eyelids test the sons of men.

[5]The LORD tests the righteous,
But the wicked and the one who loves violence His
  soul hates.
[6]Upon the wicked He will rain coals,
Fire and brimstone and a burning wind;
This shall be the portion of their cup.

**Rejoice in the Lord's righteousness and love for
the upright.**

[7]For the LORD *is* righteous,
He loves righteousness;
His countenance beholds the upright.

Psalm 12

*This is a wisdom psalm, in which David expresses his con-
fidence in the Word of God, while all around him the flattering and deceitful words of men threaten to draw God's
people away from Him. Read Romans 12:3–4.*

To the Chief Musician. On an eight-stringed harp. A Psalm of David.

**Seek God's protection from the flattering and
deceitful words of men.**

[1]Help, LORD, for the godly man ceases!
For the faithful disappear from among the sons of
  men.
[2]They speak idly everyone with his neighbor;
With flattering lips *and* a double heart they speak.

Call upon God to rise up against all the arrogant and deceitful.

[3]May the LORD cut off all flattering lips,
And the tongue that speaks proud things,
[4]Who have said,
"With our tongue we will prevail;
Our lips *are* our own;
Who *is* lord over us?"

Praise God that He rises to defend His afflicted ones.

[5]"For the oppression of the poor, for the sighing of
    the needy,
Now I will arise," says the LORD;
"I will set *him* in the safety for which he yearns."

Thank God for His Word and for His faithfulness in keeping it.

[6]The words of the LORD *are* pure words,
Like silver tried in a furnace of earth,
Purified seven times.
[7]You shall keep them, O LORD,
You shall preserve them from this generation forever.

[8]The wicked prowl on every side,
When vileness is exalted among the sons of men.

Psalm 13

*This psalm of complaint can be used in the midst of trials,
or for those who are suffering and feel cut off from the Lord.
Read 2 Corinthians 11:23–30.*

To the Chief Musician. A Psalm of David.

**Seek God's peace for yourself and for those who
suffer and are sorrowful.**

> ¹How long, O Lᴏʀᴅ?
> Will You forget me forever?
> How long will You hide Your face from me?
> ²How long shall I take counsel in my soul,
> *Having* sorrow in my heart daily?
> How long will my enemy be exalted over me?

**Pray that God may hear the prayers of those who
suffer, including yourself.**

> ³Consider *and* hear me,
> O Lᴏʀᴅ my God;
> Enlighten my eyes,
> Lest I sleep the *sleep of* death;
> ⁴Lest my enemy say,
> "I have prevailed against him";
> *Lest* those who trouble me rejoice when I am moved.

**Recall God's mercy and faithfulness, and give Him
praise.**

> ⁵But I have trusted in Your mercy;
> My heart shall rejoice in Your salvation.
> ⁶I will sing to the Lᴏʀᴅ,
> Because He has dealt bountifully with me.

Psalm 14

This psalm of complaint seeks a renewal of God's salvation among His people in the face of a generation that denies Him and troubles His people. Read Romans 1:16–23.

To the Chief Musician. *A Psalm* of David.

Deplore the arrogance and corruption of the unbelieving.

¹The fool has said in his heart,
"*There is* no God."
They are corrupt,
They have done abominable works,
There is none who does good.

Rest in God's sovereignty over this situation.

²The LORD looks down from heaven upon the
    children of men,
To see if there are any who understand, who seek
    God.
³They have all turned aside,
They have together become corrupt;
There is none who does good,
No, not one.

Rest in the Lord, who will judge the wicked.

⁴Have all the workers of iniquity no knowledge,
Who eat up my people *as* they eat bread,
And do not call on the LORD?
⁵There they are in great fear,
For God *is* with the generation of the righteous.
⁶You shame the counsel of the poor,
But the LORD is his refuge.

Pray that God will revive His people and that they will make His salvation known.

> [7]Oh, that the salvation of Israel *would come* out of
> Zion!
> When the LORD brings back the captivity of His
> people,
> Let Jacob rejoice *and* Israel be glad.

Psalm 15

This wisdom psalm teaches us to seek the righteousness of Christ and His kingdom, that we may ever dwell in the presence of the Lord. Read Matthew 6:33.

A Psalm of David.

Let the Lord examine your heart and life.

> [1]LORD, who may abide in Your tabernacle?
> Who may dwell in Your holy hill?
>
> [2]He who walks uprightly,
>   And works righteousness,
>   And speaks the truth in his heart;
> [3]He *who* does not backbite with his tongue,
>   Nor does evil to his neighbor,
>   Nor does he take up a reproach against his friend;
> [4]In whose eyes a vile person is despised,
>   But he honors those who fear the LORD;
> He *who* swears to his own hurt and does not change;
> [5]He *who* does not put out his money at usury,
>   Nor does he take a bribe against the innocent.

Express confidence in God's keeping of His just ones.

He who does these *things* shall never be moved.

Psalm 16

In this psalm of testimony, David helps us find comfort in the Lord's goodness and hope in the resurrection. As God has raised Jesus from the dead, so He will protect and raise all who trust in Him. Read Acts 2:22–33.

A Michtam of David.

Express your trust in God's saving and preserving love.

¹Preserve me, O God, for in You I put my trust.

²*O my soul,* you have said to the Lord,
"You *are* my Lord,
My goodness is nothing apart from You"—
³*And* to the saints who *are* on the earth,
"They are the excellent ones, in whom is all my
      delight."

Seek God's help in keeping you from idols.

⁴Their sorrows shall be multiplied who hasten *after*
      another *god;*
Their drink offerings of blood I will not offer,
Nor take up their names on my lips.

Rejoice in, and thank God for, His portion to you.

⁵*You,* O LORD, *are* the portion of my inheritance and
my cup;
You maintain my lot.
⁶The lines have fallen to me in pleasant *places;*
Yes, I have a good inheritance.

Bless God for His counsel.

⁷I will bless the LORD who has given me counsel;
My heart also instructs me in the night seasons.
⁸I have set the LORD always before me;
Because *He is* at my right hand I shall not be moved.

Rejoice in the hope of the resurrection.

⁹Therefore my heart is glad, and my glory rejoices.
My flesh also will rest in hope.
¹⁰For You will not leave my soul in Sheol.
Nor will You allow Your Holy One to see corruption.
¹¹You will show me the path of life;
In Your presence *is* fullness of joy;
At Your right hand *are* pleasures forevermore.

Psalm 17

*This is a psalm of testimony and imprecation. David asserts
his innocence before the Lord and calls on Him to deal with
his enemies. We can use this psalm to examine ourselves
before the Lord and rest in His wise and righteous judgment.
Read 2 Corinthians 13:1–9.*

A Prayer of David.

Let God examine your heart.

¹Hear a just cause, O LORD,
Attend to my cry;
Give ear to my prayer *that is* not from deceitful lips.
²Let my vindication come from Your presence;
Let Your eyes look on the things that are upright.

³You have tested my heart;
You have visited *me* in the night;
You have tried me and have found nothing;
I have purposed that my mouth shall not transgress.
⁴Concerning the works of men,
By the word of Your lips,
I have kept *myself* from the paths of the destroyer.
⁵Uphold my steps in Your paths,
That my footsteps may not slip.

Look to God for His favor and for protection against those who threaten you.

⁶I have called upon You, for You will hear me, O God;
Incline Your ear to me, *and* hear my speech.
⁷Show Your marvelous lovingkindness by Your right
hand,
O You who save those who trust *in You*
From those who rise up *against them.*
⁸Keep me as the apple of Your eye;
Hide me under the shadow of Your wings,
⁹From the wicked who oppress me,
From my deadly enemies who surround me.

Review the threats to your well-being, and give them to the Lord.

¹⁰They have closed up their fat *hearts;*
With their mouths they speak proudly.

¹¹They have now surrounded us in our steps.
They have set their eyes, crouching down to the
    earth,
¹²Like a lion *that* is eager to tear his prey,
And as a young lion lurking in secret places.

¹³Arise, O LORD,
Confront him, cast him down;
Deliver my life from the wicked with Your sword,
¹⁴With Your hand from men, O LORD,
From men of the world *who have* their portion in *this*
    life.
And whose belly You fill with Your hidden treasure.
They are satisfied with children,
And leave the rest of their *substance* for their babes.

**Rejoice in the prospect of seeing the Lord and
becoming more like Him.**

¹⁵As for me, I will see Your face in righteousness;
I shall be satisfied when I awake in Your likeness.

Psalm 18

*In David's psalm of praise for deliverance from his enemies
we can recall God's mercy in delivering us from sin, bask in
the righteousness of Jesus, glory in His strength, celebrate
His salvation, rest in His victory, and praise His greatness
and power. Read Philippians 3:1–21.*

To the Chief Musician. *A Psalm* of David the servant of the LORD, who spoke to the LORD the words of this song on the day that the LORD delivered him from the hand of all his enemies and from the hand of Saul. And he said:

Express your love for God, the Rock of your salvation.

¹I will love You,
   O LORD, my strength.
²The LORD is my rock and my fortress and my
   deliverer;
My God, my strength, in whom I will trust;
My shield and the horn of my salvation, my
   stronghold.
³I will call upon the LORD, *who is worthy* to be praised;
So shall I be saved from my enemies.

Recall with thanksgiving God's mercy in saving and delivering you.

⁴The pangs of death encompassed me,
And the floods of ungodliness made me afraid.
⁵The sorrows of Sheol surrounded me;
The snares of death confronted me.
⁶In my distress I called upon the LORD,
And cried out to my God;
He heard my voice from His temple,
And my cry came before Him, *even* to His ears.

⁷Then the earth shook and trembled;
The foundations of the hills also quaked and were
   shaken,
Because He was angry.
⁸Smoke went up from His nostrils,
And devouring fire from His mouth;
Coals were kindled by it.
⁹He bowed the heavens also, and came down
With darkness under His feet.
¹⁰And He rode upon a cherub, and flew;

He flew upon the wings of the wind.
¹¹He made darkness His secret place;
His canopy around Him *was* dark waters
And thick clouds of the skies.
¹²From the brightness before Him,
His thick clouds passed with hailstones and coals of
 fire.

¹³The LORD also thundered in the heavens,
And the Most High uttered His voice,
Hailstones and coals of fire.
¹⁴He sent out His arrows and scattered the foe,
Lightnings in abundance, and He vanquished them.
¹⁵Then the channels of waters were seen,
And the foundations of the world were uncovered
At Your rebuke, O LORD,
At the blast of the breath of Your nostrils.

¹⁶He sent from above, He took me;
He drew me out of many waters.
¹⁷He delivered me from my strong enemy,
From those who hated me,
For they were too strong for me.
¹⁸They confronted me in the day of my calamity,
But the LORD was my support.
¹⁹He also brought me out into a broad place;
He delivered me because He delighted in me.

**Praise God for the righteousness of Christ, which
He is bringing forth in you.**

²⁰The LORD rewarded me according to my
 righteousness;
According to the cleanness of my hands He has
 recompensed me.
²¹For I have kept the ways of the LORD,
And have not wickedly departed from my God.
²²For all His judgments *were* before me,
And I did not put away His statutes from me.

²³I was also blameless before him,
And I kept myself from my iniquity.
²⁴Therefore the Lᴏʀᴅ has recompensed me according
to my righteousness,
According to the cleanness of my hands in His sight.

Celebrate God's equitableness, uniqueness, and leading.

²⁵With the merciful
You will show Yourself merciful;
With a blameless man
You will show Yourself blameless;
²⁶With the pure
You will show Yourself pure;
And with the devious
You will show Yourself shrewd.
²⁷For You will save the humble people,
But will bring down haughty looks.

²⁸For You will light my lamp;
The Lᴏʀᴅ my God will enlighten my darkness.
²⁹For by You I can run against a troop,
And by my God I can leap over a wall.
³⁰*As for* God, His way *is* perfect;
The word of the Lᴏʀᴅ is proven;
He *is* a shield to all who trust in Him.

³¹For who *is* God, except the Lᴏʀᴅ?
And who *is* a rock, except our God?
³²*It is* God who arms me with strength,
And makes my way perfect.
³³He makes my feet like the *feet of* deer,
And sets me on my high places.
³⁴He teaches my hands to make war,
So that my arms can bend a bow of bronze.

³⁵You have also given me the shield of Your salvation;
Your right hand has held me up,
Your gentleness has made me great.
³⁶You enlarged my path under me;
So that my feet did not slip.

Rejoice in the victory and deliverance you have in Christ and in His rule over the nations.

³⁷I have pursued my enemies and overtaken them;
Neither did I turn back again till they were
    destroyed.
³⁸I have wounded them,
So that they were not able to rise;
They have fallen under my feet.
³⁹For You have armed me with strength for the battle;
You have subdued under me those who rose up
    against me.
⁴⁰You have also given me the necks of my enemies,
So that I destroyed those who hated me.
⁴¹They cried out, but *there was* none to save *them,*
Even to the LORD, but He did not answer them.
⁴²Then I beat them as fine as the dust before the
    wind;
I cast them out like dirt in the streets.

⁴³You have delivered me from the strivings of the
    people,
You have made me the head of the nations;
A people I have not known shall serve me.
⁴⁴As soon as they hear of me they obey me;
The foreigners submit to me.
⁴⁵The foreigners fade away,
And come frightened from their hideouts.

Praise and bless our glorious, saving Lord!

⁴⁶The LORD lives!
Blessed *be* my Rock!

Let the God of my salvation be exalted.
⁴⁷*It is* God who avenges me,
And subdues the peoples under me;
⁴⁸He delivers me from my enemies.
You also lift me up above those who rise up against
    me;
You have delivered me from the violent man.
⁴⁹Therefore I will give thanks to You,
    O Lᴏʀᴅ, among the Gentiles,
And sing praises to Your name.

⁵⁰Great deliverance He gives to His king,
And shows mercy to His anointed,
To David and his descendants forevermore.

Psalm 19

This psalm mixes elements of praise and testimony to cele-
brate the revelation of God in creation and His Word. Let it
guide you to meditate on the glory of God revealed there and
in the Lord Jesus Christ. Read Romans 1:18–21; Hebrews
1:1–3.

To the Chief Musician. A Psalm of David.

Praise God for His glory revealed in creation.

¹The heavens declare the glory of God;
And the firmament shows His handiwork.
²Day unto day utters speech,
And night unto night reveals knowledge.
³*There is* no speech nor language
Where their voice is not heard.
⁴Their line has gone out through all the earth,
And their words to the end of the world.
In them He has set a tabernacle for the sun,

⁵Which *is* like a bridegroom coming out of his
    chamber,
And rejoices like a strong man to run its race.
⁶Its rising *is* from one end of heaven,
And its circuit to the other end;
And there is nothing hidden from its heat.

Praise the Lord for, and seek grace to be transformed by, His perfect Word.

⁷The law of the Lᴏʀᴅ *is* perfect, converting the soul;
The testimony of the Lᴏʀᴅ *is* sure, making wise the
    simple;
⁸The statutes of the Lᴏʀᴅ *are* right, rejoicing the
    heart;
The commandment of the Lᴏʀᴅ *is* pure, enlightening
    the eyes;
⁹The fear of the Lᴏʀᴅ *is* clean, enduring forever;
The judgments of the Lᴏʀᴅ *are* true *and* righteous
    altogether.
¹⁰More to be desired *are they* than gold,
Yea, than much fine gold;
Sweeter also than honey and the honeycomb.
¹¹Moreover by them Your servant is warned,
And in keeping them *there is* great reward.

Seek grace to be free of lingering sin.

¹²Who can understand *his* errors?
Cleanse me from secret *faults.*
¹³Keep back Your servant also from presumptuous
    sins;
Let them not have dominion over me.
Then I shall be blameless,
And I shall be innocent of great transgression.

Commit your words and meditation to the Lord.

[14]Let the words of my mouth and the meditation of
my heart
Be acceptable in Your sight,
O LORD, my strength and my redeemer.

Psalm 20

*This psalm of testimony expresses David's confidence in the
Lord's saving might. Use it to seek the Lord's blessing on all
your works and ways and to declare your trust in Him. Read
Hebrews 4:14–16; Matthew 21:22.*

To the Chief Musician. A Psalm of David.

Seek God's help for all your needs.

[1]May the LORD answer you in the day of trouble;
May the name of the God of Jacob defend you;
[2]May He send you help from the sanctuary,
And strengthen you out of Zion;
[3]May He remember all your offerings,
And accept your burnt sacrifice.

Selah

[4]May He grant you according to your heart's *desire,*
And fulfill all your purpose.

Rejoice in the salvation of the Lord.

[5]We will rejoice in your salvation,
And in the name of our God we will set up *our*
banners!
May the LORD fulfill all your petitions.

Declare your trust in the saving grace of the Lord.

⁶Now I know that the LORD saves His anointed;
He will answer him from His holy heaven
With the saving strength of His right hand.

⁷Some *trust* in chariots, and some in horses;
But we will remember the name of the LORD our God.
⁸They have bowed down and fallen;
But we have risen and stand upright.

⁹Save, LORD!
May the King answer us when we call.

Psalm 21

This is a psalm of praise. David rejoices in the blessings of the Lord and declares his confidence that God will deal with his enemies. Put yourself in David's place, and join him in praising the Lord. Read Philippians 2:5–11.

To the Chief Musician. A Psalm of David.

Rejoice in the Lord's salvation and His many blessings to you.

¹The king shall have joy in Your strength, O LORD;
And in Your salvation how greatly shall he rejoice!
You have given him his heart's desire,
²And have not withheld the request of his lips.

Selah

³For You meet him with the blessings of goodness;
You set a crown of pure gold upon his head.
⁴He asked life from You, *and* You gave *it* to him—
Length of days forever and ever.

⁵His glory *is* great in Your salvation;
Honor and majesty You have placed upon him.
⁶For You have made him most blessed forever;
You have made him exceedingly glad with Your
     presence.
⁷For the king trusts in the LORD,
And through the mercy of the Most High he shall not
     be moved.

Trust in God to deliver you from and to judge all His enemies and yours.

⁸Your hand will find all Your enemies;
Your right hand will find those who hate You.
⁹You shall make them as a fiery oven in the time of
     Your anger;
The LORD shall swallow them up in His wrath,
And the fire shall devour them.
¹⁰Their offspring You shall destroy from the earth,
And their descendants from among the sons of men.
¹¹For they intended evil against You;
They devised a plot *which* they are not able *to
     perform.*
¹²Therefore You will make them turn their back;
You will make ready *Your arrows* on Your string
     toward their faces.

Exalt the Lord and praise His name!

¹³Be exalted, O LORD, in Your own strength!
We will sing and praise Your power.

Psalm 22

It is hard to miss in this psalm of testimony the saving work of Christ on the cross. Praise Him for His suffering, and for the faith He showed throughout; and praise God for vindicating Jesus and exalting Him as ruler over all the nations. Read 1 Corinthians 15:1–25; 1 Peter 2:21–24.

To the Chief Musician. Set to "The Deer of the Dawn." A Psalm of David.

Thank Jesus for suffering separation from God for you.

¹My God, My God, why have You forsaken Me?
Why are You so far from helping Me,
And from the words of My groaning?
²O My God, I cry in the daytime, but You do not hear;
And in the night season, and am not silent.

Seek from Him faith like His to bear up under all trials.

³But You *are* holy,
Who inhabit the praises of Israel.
⁴Our fathers trusted in You;
They trusted, and You delivered them.
⁵They cried to You, and were delivered;
They trusted in You, and were not ashamed.

Thank Jesus for suffering shame and reproach for you.

⁶But I *am* a worm, and no man;
A reproach of men, and despised of the people.
⁷All those who see Me laugh Me to scorn;
They shoot out the lip, they shake the head, *saying,*
⁸"He trusted in the LORD, let Him rescue Him;
Let Him deliver Him, since He delights in Him!"

Ask Jesus to help you trust as He did when trouble is upon you.

> ⁹But You *are* He who took Me out of the womb;
> You made Me trust *when I was* on My mother's
>   breasts.
> ¹⁰I was cast upon You from birth.
> From My mother's womb
> You *have been* My God.
> ¹¹Be not far from Me,
> For trouble *is* near;
> For *there is* none to help.

Thank Jesus for suffering fear, pain, and death for you.

> ¹²Many bulls have surrounded Me;
> Strong *bulls* of Bashan have encircled Me.
> ¹³They gape at Me *with* their mouths,
> *As* a raging and roaring lion.
>
> ¹⁴I am poured out like water,
> And all My bones are out of joint;
> My heart is like wax;
> It has melted within Me.
> ¹⁵My strength is dried up like a potsherd,
> And My tongue clings to My jaws;
> You have brought Me to the dust of death.
>
> ¹⁶For dogs have surrounded Me;
> The assembly of the wicked has enclosed Me.
> They pierced My hands and My feet;
> ¹⁷I can count all My bones.
> They look *and* stare at me.
> ¹⁸They divide My garments among them,
> And for My clothing they cast lots.

Seek grace to trust as Jesus did in times of deepest trial.

> [19]But You, O LORD, do not be far from Me;
> O My Strength, hasten to help Me!
> [20]Deliver Me from the sword,
> My precious *life* from the power of the dog.
> [21]Save Me from the lion's mouth
> And from the horns of the wild oxen!

Praise God that He answered Jesus' prayer, vindicated Him, and raised Him, so that through Him we might know and praise the Lord.

> You have answered Me.

> [22]I will declare Your name to My brethren;
> In the midst of the congregation I will praise You.
> [23]You who fear the LORD, praise Him!
> All you descendants of Jacob, glorify Him!
> And fear Him, all you offspring of Israel!
> [24]For He has not despised nor abhorred the affliction
>   of the afflicted;
> Nor has He hidden His face from Him;
> But when He cried to Him, He heard.

> [25]My praise *shall be* of You in the great congregation;
> I will pay My vows before those who fear Him.
> [26]The poor shall eat and be satisfied;
> Those who seek Him will praise the LORD.
> Let your heart live forever!

Celebrate the mighty rule of Jesus!

> [27]All the ends of the world
> Shall remember and turn to the LORD,
> And all the families of the nations
> Shall worship before You.

²⁸For the kingdom *is* the Lord's,
And He rules over the nations.

²⁹All the prosperous of the earth
Shall eat and worship;
All those who go down to the dust
Shall bow before Him,
Even he who cannot keep himself alive.

³⁰A posterity shall serve Him.
It will be recounted of the Lord to the *next*
     generation,
³¹They will come and declare His righteousness to a
     people who will be born,
That He has done *this*.

Psalm 23

*This psalm of testimony is by far the most beloved. Praise
our great Shepherd and recount His many blessings to you.
Read John 10:11–17.*

A Psalm of David.

Declare your trust in Jesus, and name His many blessings.

¹The Lord *is* my shepherd;
I shall not want.
²He makes me to lie down in green pastures;
He leads me beside the still waters.
³He restores my soul;
He leads me in the paths of righteousness
For His name's sake.

Celebrate the presence of Jesus and His protection from all enemies.

⁴Yea, though I walk through the valley of the shadow
    of death,
I will fear no evil;
For You *are* with me;
Your rod and Your staff, they comfort me.
⁵You prepare a table before me in the presence of my
    enemies;
You anoint my head with oil;
My cup runs over.

Praise the Lord for His constant goodness and for the gift of eternal life.

⁶Surely goodness and mercy shall follow me
All the days of my life;
And I will dwell in the house of the LORD
Forever.

Psalm 24

In this testimony psalm David proclaims the Lord's rule and meditates on the qualifications of those who would dwell with Him. Thank God for the righteousness of Christ, and seek grace for sanctification. Read Romans 8:1–11.

A Psalm of David.

Celebrate God's mighty rule over the creation.

¹The earth *is* the LORD's, and all its fullness,
The world and those who dwell therein.
²For He has founded it upon the seas,
And established it upon the waters.

Seek God's grace for sanctification, that you may dwell in His presence forever.

³Who may ascend into the hill of the LORD?
Or who may stand in His holy place?
⁴He who has clean hands and a pure heart,
Who has not lifted up his soul to an idol,
Nor sworn deceitfully.
⁵He shall receive blessing from the LORD,
And righteousness from the God of his salvation.
⁶This *is* Jacob, the generation of those who seek Him,
Who seek Your face.

Selah

Open wide the gates of your life to the mighty, sanctifying presence of the Lord.

⁷Lift up your heads, O you gates!
And be lifted up, you everlasting doors!
And the King of glory shall come in.
⁸Who *is* this King of glory?
The LORD strong and mighty,
The LORD mighty in battle.
⁹Lift up your heads, O you gates!
And lift *them* up, you everlasting doors!
And the King of glory shall come in.
¹⁰Who is this King of glory?
The LORD of hosts,
He *is* the King of glory.

Selah

Psalm 25

This psalm contains elements of complaint, testimony, and praise. It can be especially helpful in times of distress, or in praying for those who are experiencing trouble. Read Ephesians 6:10–20.

A *Psalm* of David.

Declare your confidence in God in the face of enemies.

¹To You, O LORD, I lift up my soul.
²O my God, I trust in You;
Let me not be ashamed;
Let not my enemies triumph over me.
³Indeed, let no one who waits on You be ashamed.
Let those be ashamed who deal treacherously without
   cause.

Seek God's counsel, kindness, and mercy in your time of need.

⁴Show me Your ways, O LORD;
Teach me Your paths.
⁵Lead me in Your truth and teach me,
For You *are* the God of my salvation;
On You I wait all the day.

⁶Remember, O LORD, Your tender mercies and Your
   lovingkindnesses,
For they *have been* from of old.
⁷Do not remember the sins of my youth, nor my
   transgressions;
According to Your mercy remember me,
For Your goodness' sake, O LORD.

Praise the goodness of the Lord, and ask His help for leading a life that is pleasing to Him.

⁸Good and upright *is* the Lord;
Therefore He teaches sinners in the way.
⁹The humble He guides in justice,
And the humble He teaches His way.
¹⁰All the paths of the Lord *are* mercy and truth,
To such as keep His covenant and His testimonies.
¹¹For Your name's sake, O Lord,
Pardon my iniquity, for it *is* great.

Claim the promises of God's covenant.

¹²Who *is* the man that fears the Lord?
Him shall He teach in the way He chooses.
¹³He himself shall dwell in prosperity,
And his descendants shall inherit the earth.
¹⁴The secret of the Lord *is* with those who fear Him,
And He will show them His covenant.
¹⁵My eyes *are* ever toward the Lord,
For He shall pluck my feet out of the net.

Seek mercy and deliverance from all troubles.

¹⁶Turn Yourself to me, and have mercy on me,
For I *am* desolate and afflicted.
¹⁷The troubles of my heart have enlarged;
Oh, bring me out of my distresses!
¹⁸Look on my affliction and my pain,
And forgive all my sins.
¹⁹Consider my enemies, for they are many;
And they hate me with cruel hatred.
²⁰Oh, keep my soul, and deliver me;
Let me not be ashamed, for I put my trust in You.
²¹Let integrity and uprightness preserve me,
For I wait for You.
²²Redeem Israel, O God,
Out of all their troubles!

Psalm 26

Use this psalm of complaint to examine yourself before the Lord and to seek His help in following His path. Read Galatians 6:1–5.

A Psalm of David.

Allow the Lord to examine your heart, mind, and life.

¹Vindicate me, O LORD,
For I have walked in my integrity.
I have also trusted in the LORD;
I shall not slip.
²Examine me, O LORD, and prove me;
Try my mind and my heart.
³For Your lovingkindness *is* before my eyes,
And I have walked in Your truth.
⁴I have not sat with idolatrous mortals,
Nor will I go in with hypocrites.
⁵I have hated the congregation of evildoers,
And will not sit with the wicked.

Resolve to thank, proclaim, and love the Lord.

⁶I will wash my hands in innocence;
So I will go about Your altar, O LORD,
⁷That I may proclaim with the voice of thanksgiving,
And tell of Your wondrous works.
⁸LORD, I have loved the habitation of Your house,
And the place where Your glory dwells.

Seek God's help in following Him.

⁹Do not gather my soul *together* with sinners,
Nor my life with bloodthirsty men,
¹⁰In whose hands *is* a sinister scheme,
And whose right hand is full of bribes.

¹¹But as for me, I will walk in my integrity;
Redeem me and be merciful to me.
¹²My foot stands in an even place;
In the congregations I will bless the LORD.

Psalm 27

This is a psalm of testimony. Declare your confidence in the Lord, your determination to serve and follow Him, and your expectation that His goodness will be your aim. Read 2 Peter 1:5–11.

A Psalm of David.

Express your confidence in the Lord.

¹The LORD *is* my light and my salvation;
Whom shall I fear?
The LORD *is* the strength of my life;
Of whom shall I be afraid?
²When the wicked came against me
To eat up my flesh,
My enemies and foes,
They stumbled and fell.
³Though an army should encamp against me,
My heart shall not fear;
Though war should rise against me,
In this I *will be* confident.

Seek the presence and protection of the Lord.

⁴One *thing* I have desired of the LORD,
That I will seek:
That I may dwell in the house of the LORD
All the days of my life,

To behold the beauty of the LORD,
And to inquire in His temple.
⁵For in the time of trouble
He shall hide me in His pavilion;
In the secret place of His tabernacle
He shall hide me;
He shall set me high upon a rock.

⁶And now my head shall be lifted up above my
  enemies all around me;
Therefore I will offer sacrifices of joy in His
  tabernacle;
I will sing, yes, I will sing praises to the LORD.

⁷Hear, O LORD, *when* I cry with my voice!
Have mercy also upon me, and answer me.

Ask God to help you to obey Him and to realize His constant presence.

⁸*When You said,* "Seek My face,"
My heart said to You, "Your face, LORD, I will seek."
⁹Do not hide Your face from me;
Do not turn Your servant away in anger;
You have been my help;
Do not leave me nor forsake me,
O God of my salvation.
¹⁰When my father and my mother forsake me,
Then the LORD will take care of me.

Seek the Lord's will and His goodness. Resolve to wait on Him.

¹¹Teach me Your way, O LORD,
And lead me in a smooth path, because of my
  enemies.
¹²Do not deliver me to the will of my adversaries;
For false witnesses have risen against me,

And such as breathe out violence.
¹³*I would have lost heart,* unless I had believed
That I would see the goodness of the LORD
In the land of the living.

¹⁴Wait on the LORD;
Be of good courage,
And He shall strengthen your heart;
Wait, I say, on the LORD!

Psalm 28

Let David's words of praise and testimony be your own as you seek the Lord's help in resisting temptation. Read 2 Corinthians 10:13.

A Psalm of David.

Plead with God to hear your prayers.

¹To You I will cry, O LORD my Rock:
Do not be silent to me,
Lest, if You *are* silent to me,
I become like those who go down to the pit.
²Hear the voice of my supplications
When I cry to You,
When I lift up my hands toward Your holy sanctuary.

Seek protection against temptation and His justice against the wicked.

³Do not take me away with the wicked
And with the workers of iniquity,
Who speak peace to their neighbors
But evil *is* in their hearts.

⁴Give to them according to their deeds,
And according to the wickedness of their endeavors;
Give to them according to the work of their hands;
Render to them what they deserve.
⁵Because they do not regard the works of the Lord,
Nor the operation of His hands,
He shall destroy them
And not build them up.

Praise the Lord, who hears your prayers.

⁶Blessed *be* the Lord,
Because He has heard the voice of my supplications!
⁷The Lord *is* my strength and my shield;
My heart trusted in Him, and I am helped;
Therefore my heart greatly rejoices,
And with my song I will praise Him.

Declare your confidence in God's saving strength.

⁸The Lord *is* their strength,
And He is the saving refuge of His anointed.
⁹Save Your people,
And bless Your inheritance;
Shepherd them also,
And bear them up forever.

Psalm 29

David praises the glory of the Lord and the power of His Word. Rejoice with him in God's sovereign, unshakable rule. Read Revelation 11:15–19.

A Psalm of David.

Give glory to God for His beauty and strength.

¹Give unto the LORD,
    O you mighty ones,
Give unto the LORD glory and strength.
²Give unto the LORD the glory due to His name;
Worship the LORD in the beauty of holiness.

Praise the Lord, who rules the world by His sovereign Word.

³The voice of the LORD *is* over the waters;
The God of glory thunders;
The LORD *is* over many waters.
⁴The voice of the LORD *is* powerful;
The voice of the LORD *is* full of majesty.

⁵The voice of the LORD breaks the cedars,
Yes, the LORD splinters the cedars of Lebanon.
⁶He makes them also skip like a calf,
Lebanon and Sirion like a young wild ox.
⁷The voice of the LORD divides the flames of fire.

⁸The voice of the LORD shakes the wilderness;
The LORD shakes the Wilderness of Kadesh.
⁹The voice of the LORD makes the deer give birth,
And strips the forests bare;
And in His temple everyone says, "Glory!"

Praise the Lord, enthroned on high.

¹⁰The LORD sat *enthroned* at the Flood,
And the LORD sits as King forever.
¹¹The LORD will give strength to His people;
The LORD will bless His people with peace.

Psalm 30

With David, praise the Lord in the midst of chastening, for His mercy and renewing grace are ever at hand. Read Hebrews 12:3–11.

A Psalm. A Song at the dedication of the house of David.

Praise God for His healing grace.

¹I will extol You, O LORD, for You have lifted me up,
And have not let my foes rejoice over me.
²O LORD my God, I cried out to You,
And You have healed me.
³O LORD, You have brought my soul up from the
    grave;
You have kept me alive, that I should not go down to
    the pit.

Praise the Lord that His chastening leads to renewal.

⁴Sing praise to the LORD, You saints of His,
And give thanks at the remembrance of His holy
    name.
⁵For His anger *is but for* a moment,
His favor *is for* life;
Weeping may endure for a night,
But joy *comes* in the morning.
⁶Now in my prosperity I said,
"I shall never be moved."
⁷LORD, by Your favor You have made my mountain
    stand strong;
You hid Your face, *and* I was troubled.

⁸I cried out to You, O LORD;
And to the LORD I made supplication:

⁹"What profit *is there* in my blood,
When I go down to the pit?
Will the dust praise You?
Will it declare Your truth?
¹⁰Hear, O Lᴏʀᴅ, and have mercy on me;
Lᴏʀᴅ, be my helper!"

Give praise and thanks to God for His renewing grace.

¹¹You have turned for me my mourning into dancing;
You have put off my sackcloth and clothed me with
    gladness,
¹²To the end that *my* glory may sing praise to You and
    not be silent.
O Lᴏʀᴅ my God, I will give thanks to You forever.

Psalm 31

This psalm of complaint, testimony, and praise must surely have been on the Lord Jesus' mind as He suffered for us (cf. v. 5). Use it to renew your faith or to intercede for others in the midst of trial. Read 2 Corinthians 11:22–31.

To the Chief Musician. A Psalm of David.

Declare your confidence in the Lord, and seek His help in times of trouble.

¹In You, O Lᴏʀᴅ, I put my trust;
Let me never be ashamed;
Deliver me in Your righteousness.
²Bow down Your ear to me,
Deliver me speedily;
Be my rock of refuge,
A fortress of defense to save me.

³For You *are* my rock and my fortress;
Therefore, for Your name's sake,
Lead me and guide me.
⁴Pull me out of the net which they have
    secretly laid for me,
For You *are* my strength.
⁵Into Your hand I commit my spirit;
You have redeemed me,
    O Lord God of truth.

Present your troubles, or those of others, to the Lord.

⁶I have hated those who regard vain
    idols;
But I trust in the Lord.
⁷I will be glad
    and rejoice in Your mercy,
For You have considered my trouble;
You have known my soul in
    adversities,
⁸And have not shut me up into the
    hand of the enemy;
You have set my feet in a wide place.

⁹Have mercy on me, O Lord, for I am in trouble;
My eye wastes away with grief,
Yes, my soul and my body!
¹⁰For my life is spent with grief,
And my years with sighing;
My strength fails because of my iniquity,
And my bones waste away.
¹¹I am a reproach among all my enemies,
But especially among my neighbors,
And *am* repulsive to my acquaintances;
Those who see me outside flee from me.
¹²I am forgotten like a dead man, out of mind;

I am like a broken vessel.
¹³For I hear the slander of many;
Fear *is* on every side;
While they take counsel together against me,
They scheme to take away my life.

Renew your trust and hope in the Lord.

¹⁴But as for me, I trust in You, O LORD;
I say, "You *are* my God."
¹⁵My times *are* in Your hand;
Deliver me from the hand of my enemies,
And from those who persecute me.
¹⁶Make Your face shine upon Your servant;
Save me for Your mercies' sake.
¹⁷Do not let me be ashamed, O LORD, for I have called
   upon You;
Let the wicked be ashamed;
Let them be silent in the grave.
¹⁸Let the lying lips be put to silence,
Which speak insolent things proudly and
   contemptuously against the righteous.

Praise the goodness, mercy, and kindness of the Lord, and declare your love for Him.

¹⁹Oh, how great *is* Your goodness,
Which You have laid up for those who fear You,
Which You have prepared for those who trust in You
In the presence of the sons of men!
²⁰You shall hide them in the secret place of Your
   presence
From the plots of man;
You shall keep them secretly in a pavilion
From the strife of tongues.

²¹Blessed *be* the LORD,
For He has shown me His marvelous kindness in a
    strong city!
²²For I said in my haste,
"I am cut off from before Your eyes";
Nevertheless You heard the voice of my supplications
When I cried to You.
²³Oh, love the LORD, all you His saints!
For the LORD preserves the faithful,
And fully repays the proud person.
²⁴Be of good courage,
And He shall strengthen your heart,
All you who hope in the LORD.

Psalm 32

This psalm is appropriate for daily confession of sin, but espe-cially when the hand of the Lord is weighing on you with con-viction. Read John 16:8; 1 John 1:8–9.

A Psalm of David. A Contemplation.

Praise God for forgiving grace.

¹Blessed *is he whose* transgression *is* forgiven,
Whose sin *is* covered.
²Blessed *is* the man to whom the LORD does not
    impute iniquity,
And in whose spirit *there is* no guile.

**Acknowledge the convicting power of God's Spirit,
and confess your sins.**

³When I kept silent, my bones grew old
Through my groaning all the day long.

⁴For day and night Your hand was heavy upon me;
My vitality was turned into the drought of summer.

                    Selah

⁵I acknowledged my sin to You,
And my iniquity I have not hidden.
I said, "I will confess my transgressions to the LORD,"
And You forgave the iniquity of my sin.

                    Selah

Express confidence in the deliverance and leading of the Lord.

⁶For this cause everyone who is godly shall pray to
    You
In a time when You may be found;
Surely in a flood of great waters
They shall not come near him.
⁷You *are* my hiding place;
You shall preserve me from trouble;
You shall surround me with songs of deliverance.

                    Selah

⁸I will instruct you and teach you in the way you
    should go;
I will guide you with My eye.
⁹Do not be like the horse *or* like the mule,
Which have no understanding,
Which must be harnessed with bit and bridle,
Else they will not come near you.

¹⁰Many sorrows *shall be* to the wicked;
But he who trusts in the LORD, mercy shall surround
    him.
¹¹Be glad in the LORD and rejoice, you righteous;
And shout for joy, all *you* upright in heart!

Psalm 33

This is a psalm of testimony, celebrating the power of God's Word, His sovereignty over the nations, and His grace and care for those who fear Him. Use it to renew your faith in the Lord. Read Ephesians 3:14–21.

Praise God for His mighty, sovereign Word and His good and righteous works.

¹Rejoice in the LORD, O you righteous!
For praise from the upright is beautiful.
²Praise the LORD with the harp;
Make melody to Him with an instrument of ten
    strings.
³Sing to Him a new song;
Play skillfully with a shout of joy.

⁴For the word of the LORD *is* right,
And all His work *is done* in truth.
⁵He loves righteousness and justice;
The earth is full of the goodness of the LORD.

Testify of God's powerful, faithful Word.

⁶By the word of the LORD the heavens were made,
And all the host of them by the breath of His mouth.
⁷He gathers the waters of the sea together as a heap;
He lays up the deep in storehouses.

⁸Let all the earth fear the LORD;
Let all the inhabitants of the world stand in awe of
    Him.
⁹For He spoke, and it was *done;*
He commanded, and it stood fast.

¹⁰The LORD brings the counsel of the nations to
    nothing;

He makes the plans of the peoples of no effect.
^{11}The counsel of the LORD stands forever,
The plans of His heart to all generations.
^{12}Blessed *is* the nation whose God *is* the LORD,
And the people *whom* He has chosen as His own
    inheritance.

Rehearse the sovereignty of God and His saving mercy.

^{13}The LORD looks from heaven;
He sees all the sons of men.
^{14}From the place of His habitation He looks
On all the inhabitants of the earth;
^{15}He fashions their hearts individually;
He considers all their works.

^{16}No king *is* saved by the multitude of an army;
A mighty man is not delivered by great strength.
^{17}A horse *is* a vain hope for safety;
Neither shall it deliver *any* by its great strength.

^{18}Behold, the eye of the LORD *is* on those who fear
    Him,
On those who hope in His mercy,
^{19}To deliver their soul from death,
And to keep them alive in famine.

Wait on the Lord, and rejoice in Him.

^{20}Our soul waits for the LORD;
He *is* our help and our shield.
^{21}For our heart shall rejoice in Him,
Because we have trusted in His holy name.
^{22}Let Your mercy, O LORD, be upon us,
Just as we hope in You.

Psalm 34

In this wisdom psalm David recommends the way of the righteous who, trusting in the Lord, are listened to, led, and cared for by Him. The psalm points us to the ultimate righteousness of Christ (vv. 19–20) and encourages us to seek the Lord and His ways. Read Matthew 6:25–34.

A *Psalm* of David when he pretended madness before Abimelech, who drove him away, and he departed.

Praise the Lord, who hears the prayers of His people.

¹I will bless the LORD at all times;
His praise *shall* continually *be* in my mouth.
²My soul shall make its boast in the LORD;
The humble shall hear *of it* and be glad.
³Oh, magnify the LORD with me,
And let us exalt His name together.

⁴I sought the LORD, and He heard me,
And delivered me from all my fears.
⁵They looked to Him and were radiant,
And their faces were not ashamed.
⁶This poor man cried out, and the LORD heard *him,*
And saved him out of all his troubles.
⁷The angel of the LORD encamps all around those who
     fear Him,
And delivers them.

Seek the Lord, to fear Him and to desire His way.

⁸Oh, taste and see that the LORD *is* good;
Blessed *is* the man *who* trusts in Him!
⁹Oh, fear the LORD, you His saints!
There is no want to those who fear Him.

¹⁰The young lions lack and suffer hunger;
But those who seek the LORD shall not lack any good
    thing.

¹¹Come, you children, listen to me;
I will teach you the fear of the LORD.
¹²Who *is* the man *who* desires life,
And loves *many* days, that he may see good?
¹³Keep your tongue from evil,
And your lips from speaking guile.
¹⁴Depart from evil, and do good;
Seek peace, and pursue it.

Thank God that He watches over us, hears our prayers, and delivers us from afflictions.

¹⁵The eyes of the LORD *are* on the righteous,
And His ears *are open* to their cry.
¹⁶The face of the LORD *is* against those who do evil,
To cut off the remembrance of them from the earth.

¹⁷*The righteous* cry out, and the LORD hears,
And delivers them out of all their troubles.
¹⁸The LORD *is* near to those who have a broken heart,
And saves such as have a contrite spirit.

¹⁹Many *are* the afflictions of the righteous,
But the LORD delivers him out of them all.
²⁰He guards all his bones;
Not one of them is broken.
²¹Evil shall slay the wicked,
And those who hate the righteous shall be
    condemned.
²²The LORD redeems the soul of His servants,
And none of those who trust in Him shall be
    condemned.

Psalm 35

In this psalm of complaint David calls on the Lord to deliver him from his foes. Pray for the persecuted church, as well as for yourself and any who are under oppression of any kind. Read 1 Peter 1:3–9.

A Psalm of David.

Call upon God to resist the enemies of His people.

¹Plead *my cause,* O LORD, with those who strive with
    me;
Fight against those who fight against me.
²Take hold of shield and buckler,
And stand up for my help.
³Also draw out the spear,
And stop those who pursue me.
Say to my soul,
"I *am* your salvation."

⁴Let those be put to shame and brought to dishonor
Who seek after my life;
Let those be turned back and brought to confusion
Who plot my hurt.
⁵Let them be like chaff before the wind,
And let the angel of the LORD chase *them.*
⁶Let their way be dark and slippery,
And let the angel of the LORD pursue them.
⁷For without cause they have hidden their net for me
    in a pit,
Which they have dug without cause for my life.
⁸Let destruction come upon him unexpectedly,
And let his net that he has hidden catch himself;
Into that very destruction let him fall.

Rejoice in the Lord's deliverance.

⁹And my soul shall be joyful in the LORD;
It shall rejoice in His salvation.
¹⁰All my bones shall say,
"LORD, who *is* like You,
Delivering the poor from him who is too strong for
    him,
Yes, the poor and the needy from him who plunders
    him?"

In David's affliction—and Christ's—rehearse your own troubles, and present them to the Lord.

¹¹Fierce witnesses rise up;
They ask me *things* that I do not know.
¹²They reward me evil for good,
To the sorrow of my soul.
¹³But as for me, when they were sick,
My clothing *was* sackcloth;
I humbled myself with fasting;
And my prayer would return to my own heart.
¹⁴I paced about as though *he were* my friend *or*
    brother;
I bowed down heavily, as one who mourns *for his*
    mother.

¹⁵But in my adversity they rejoiced
And gathered together;
Attackers gathered against me,
And I did not know *it*;
They tore *at me* and did not cease;
¹⁶With ungodly mockers at feasts
They gnashed at me with their teeth.

Seek the Lord's deliverance from your trials and His victory over your foes.

¹⁷Lord, how long will You look on?
Rescue me from their destructions,
My precious *life* from the lions.
¹⁸I will give You thanks in the great congregation;
I will praise You among many people.

¹⁹Let them not rejoice over me who are wrongfully
  my enemies;
Nor let them wink with the eye who hate me without
  a cause.
²⁰For they do not speak peace,
But they devise deceitful matters
Against *those who are* quiet in the land.
²¹They also opened their mouth wide against me,
And said, "Aha, aha!
Our eyes have seen *it*."

²²*This* You have seen, O Lord;
Do not keep silence.
O Lord, do not be far from me.
²³Stir up Yourself, and awaken to my vindication,
To my cause, my God and my Lord.
²⁴Vindicate me, O Lord my God, according to Your
  righteousness;
And let them not rejoice over me.
²⁵Let them not say in their hearts,
    "Ah, so we would have it!"
Let them not say,
    "We have swallowed him up."

²⁶Let them be ashamed and brought to mutual
  confusion
Who rejoice at my hurt;
Let them be clothed with shame and dishonor
Who magnify themselves against me.

Give praise to God for His care for His people.

²⁷Let them shout for joy and be glad,
Who favor my righteous cause;
And let them say continually,
"Let the LORD be magnified,
Who has pleasure in the prosperity of His servant."
²⁸And my tongue shall speak of Your righteousness
And of Your praise all day long.

Psalm 36

*In this wisdom psalm David teaches us to seek the goodness
of the Lord and to despise the way of the wicked. Read Galatians 5:16–25.*

To the Chief Musician. *A Psalm* of David the servant of the LORD.

Deplore the way of the wicked.

¹An oracle within my heart concerning the
    transgression of the wicked:
There is no fear of God before his eyes.
²For he flatters himself in his own eyes,
When he finds out his iniquity *and* when he hates.
³The words of his mouth *are* wickedness and deceit;
He has ceased to be wise *and* to do good.
⁴He devises wickedness on his bed;
He sets himself in a way *that is* not good.
He does not abhor evil.

Celebrate and seek the goodness of the Lord.

⁵Your mercy, O LORD, *is* in the heavens,
And Your faithfulness *reaches* to the clouds.

⁶Your righteousness *is* like the great mountains;
Your judgments *are* a great deep;
O Lᴏʀᴅ, You preserve man and beast.
⁷How precious *is* Your lovingkindness, O God!
Therefore the children of men put their trust under
the shadow of Your wings.
⁸They are abundantly satisfied with the fullness of
Your house,
And You give them drink from the river of Your
pleasures.
⁹For with You *is* the fountain of life;
In Your light we see light.

**Resolve to seek the way of the Lord; pray for the
wicked.**

¹⁰Oh, continue Your lovingkindness to those who
know You,
And Your righteousness to the upright in heart.
¹¹Let not the foot of pride come against me,
And let not the hand of the wicked drive me away.
¹²There the workers of iniquity have fallen;
They have been cast down and are not able to rise.

Psalm 37

*In this wisdom psalm David counsels us to trust in the Lord
in the presence of the wicked, to delight in and wait on Him,
and to rest in His salvation. Use this psalm to renew your
confidence in the Lord in the face of daily temptations and
trials. Read Romans 8:1–11.*

A Psalm of David.

Do not be anxious over the wicked; trust in the Lord, and rest in Him.

[1]Do not fret because of evildoers,
Nor be envious of the workers of iniquity.
[2]For they shall soon be cut down like the grass,
And wither as the green herb.

[3]Trust in the LORD, and do good;
Dwell in the land, and feed on His faithfulness.
[4]Delight yourself also in the LORD,
And He shall give you the desires of your heart.

[5]Commit your way to the LORD,
Trust also in Him.
And He shall bring *it* to pass.
[6]He shall bring forth your righteousness as the light,
And your justice as the noonday.

[7]Rest in the LORD, and wait patiently for Him;
Do not fret because of him who prospers in his way,
Because of the man who brings wicked schemes to
    pass.
[8]Cease from anger, and forsake wrath;
Do not fret—*it* only *causes* harm.
[9]For evildoers shall be cut off;
But those who wait on the LORD,
They shall inherit the earth.
[10]For yet a little while and the wicked *shall be* no
    more;
Indeed, you will look diligently for his place,
But it *shall be* no *more.*
[11]But the meek shall inherit the earth,
And shall delight themselves in the abundance of
    peace.

Commit to follow the way of the righteous and to shun the wicked path.

¹²The wicked plots against the just,
And gnashes at him with his teeth.
¹³The Lord laughs at him,
For He sees that his day is coming.
¹⁴The wicked have drawn the sword
And have bent their bow,
To cast down the poor and needy,
To slay those who are of upright conduct.
¹⁵Their sword shall enter their own heart,
And their bows shall be broken.

¹⁶A little that a righteous man has
Is better than the riches of many wicked.
¹⁷For the arms of the wicked shall be broken,
But the Lord upholds the righteous.

¹⁸The Lord knows the days of the upright,
And their inheritance shall be forever.
¹⁹They shall not be ashamed in the evil time,
And in the days of famine they shall be satisfied.
²⁰But the wicked shall perish;
And the enemies of the Lord,
Like the splendor of the meadows, shall vanish.
Into smoke they shall vanish away.

²¹The wicked borrows and does not repay,
But the righteous shows mercy and gives.
²²For *those who are* blessed by Him shall inherit the
  earth,
But *those who are* cursed by Him shall be cut off.

²³The steps of a *good* man are ordered by the Lord,
And He delights in his way.
²⁴Though he fall, he shall not be utterly cast down;
For the Lord upholds *him with* His hand.

²⁵I have been young, and *now* am old;
Yet I have not seen the righteous forsaken,
Nor his descendants begging bread.
²⁶*He is* ever merciful, and lends;
And his descendants *are* blessed.

²⁷Depart from evil, and do good;
And dwell forevermore.
²⁸For the LORD loves justice,
And does not forsake His saints;
They are preserved forever,
But the descendants of the wicked shall be cut off.
²⁹The righteous shall inherit the land,
And dwell in it forever.

³⁰The mouth of the righteous speaks wisdom,
And his tongue talks of justice.
³¹The law of his God *is* in his heart;
None of his steps shall slide.

³²The wicked watches the righteous,
And seeks to slay him.
³³The LORD will not leave him in his hand,
Nor condemn him when he is judged.

Wait on the Lord, and rest in His strength and salvation.

³⁴Wait on the LORD,
And keep His way,
And He shall exalt you to inherit the land;
When the wicked are cut off, you shall see *it*.
³⁵I have seen the wicked in great power,
And spreading himself like a native green tree.
³⁶Yet he passed away, and behold, he *was* no *more;*
Indeed I sought him, but he could not be found.

³⁷Mark the blameless *man*, and observe the upright;
For the future of *that* man *is* peace.
³⁸But the transgressors shall be destroyed together;
The future of the wicked shall be cut off.

³⁹But the salvation of the righteous *is* from the LORD;
He is their strength in the time of trouble.
⁴⁰And the LORD shall help them and deliver them;
He shall deliver them from the wicked,
And save them,
Because they trust in Him.

Psalm 38

Use this psalm of confession to consider the harmful effects of unconfessed sin, and to seek repentance and renewal for yourself and all of God's people. Read Romans 6:15–23.

A Psalm of David. To bring to remembrance.

Allow God's Spirit to convict you of any unacknowledged sin.

¹O LORD, do not rebuke me in Your wrath,
Nor chasten me in Your hot displeasure!
²For Your arrows pierce me deeply,
And Your hand presses me down.

³*There is* no soundness in my flesh
Because of Your anger,
Nor *is there any* health in my bones
Because of my sin.
⁴For my iniquities have gone over my head;
Like a heavy burden they are too heavy for me.
⁵My wounds are foul *and* festering
Because of my foolishness.

⁶I am troubled, I am bowed down greatly;
I go mourning all the day long.
⁷For my loins are full of inflammation,
And *there is* no soundness in my flesh.
⁸I am feeble and severely broken;
I groan because of the turmoil of my heart.

Seek the forgiving, renewing grace of the Lord.

⁹Lord, all my desire *is* before You;
And my sighing is not hidden from You.
¹⁰My heart pants, my strength fails me;
As for the light of my eyes, it also has gone from me.

¹¹My loved ones and my friends stand aloof from my
    plague,
And my kinsmen stand afar off.
¹²Those also who seek my life lay snares *for me;*
Those who seek my hurt speak of destruction,
And plan deception all the day long.

Pray that God will make you deaf to temptation, that you may seek Him.

¹³But I, like a deaf *man,* do not hear;
And *I am* like a mute *who* does not open his mouth.
¹⁴Thus I am like a man who does not hear,
And in whose mouth *is* no response.

¹⁵For in You, O Lᴏʀᴅ, I hope;
You will hear, O Lord my God.
¹⁶For I said, "*Hear me,* lest they rejoice over me,
Lest, when my foot slips, they magnify *themselves*
    against me."

Confess your sin and hope in the Lord.

¹⁷For I *am* ready to fall,
And my sorrow *is* continually before me.

¹⁸For I will declare my iniquity;
I will be in anguish over my sin.
¹⁹But my enemies *are* vigorous, *and* they are strong;
And those who hate me wrongfully have multiplied.
²⁰Those also who render evil for good,
They are my adversaries, because I follow *what is*
good.

²¹Do not forsake me, O LORD;
O my God, be not far from me!
²²Make haste to help me,
O Lord, my salvation!

Psalm 39

*This psalm has elements of confession (vv. 2–3), testimony
(vv. 7–11), and complaint (vv. 4–6, 12–13). David seems
concerned to make sure his life, fleeting though it is, counts
for the Lord, and we can use his words to seek that as well.
Read James 4:7–17.*

To the Chief Musician. To Jeduthun. A Psalm of David.

**Consider whether your words—and your life—are
as fully invested for the Lord as they might be.**

¹I said, "I will guard my ways,
Lest I sin with my tongue;
I will restrain my mouth with a muzzle,
While the wicked are before me."
²I was mute with silence,
I held my peace *even* from good;
And my sorrow was stirred up.

³My heart was hot within me;
While I was musing, the fire burned.
Then I spoke with my tongue:

Renew your resolve to live each day fully for the Lord.

⁴"LORD, make me to know my end,
And what *is* the measure of my days,
That I may know how frail I *am*.
⁵Indeed, You have made my days *as* handbreadths,
And my age *is* as nothing before You;
Certainly every man at his best state *is* but vapor.

Selah

⁶Surely every man walks about like a shadow;
Surely they busy themselves in vain;
He heaps up *riches,*
And does not know who will gather them.

Hope in the Lord for forgiveness and renewing grace.

⁷"And now, Lord, what do I wait for?
My hope *is* in You.
⁸Deliver me from all my transgressions;
Do not make me the reproach of the foolish.
⁹I was mute, I did not open my mouth,
Because it was You who did *it.*
¹⁰Remove Your plague from me;
I am consumed by the blow of Your hand.
¹¹When with rebukes You correct man for iniquity,
You make his beauty melt away like a moth;
Surely every man *is* vapor.

Selah

¹²"Hear my prayer, O LORD,
And give ear to my cry;
Do not be silent at my tears;

For I *am* a stranger with You,
A sojourner, as all my fathers *were*.
[13]Remove Your gaze from me, that I may regain
  strength,
Before I go away and am no more."

Psalm 40

*This is a psalm of testimony and complaint. David confesses
his trust and hope in the Lord and seeks deliverance from
unspecified evils. This is a wonderful psalm for reviewing
God's saving mercy and seeking His help for daily persever-
ance in the faith. Read 1 John 4:1–19.*

To the Chief Musician. A Psalm of David.

**Praise the Lord for His mercy in delivering grace,
for His calling, and for His many works on your
behalf.**

[1]I waited patiently for the LORD;
And He inclined to me,
And heard my cry.
[2]He also brought me up out of a horrible pit,
Out of the miry clay,
And set my feet upon a rock,
And established my steps.
[3]He has put a new song in my mouth—
Praise to our God;
Many will see *it* and fear,
And will trust in the LORD.

[4]Blessed *is* that man who makes the LORD his trust,
And does not respect the proud, nor such as turn
  aside to lies.

⁵Many, O LORD my God, *are* Your wonderful works
Which You have done;
And Your thoughts *which are* toward us
Cannot be recounted to You in order;
If I would declare and speak *of them,*
They are more than can be numbered.

Commit your life anew to the Lord.

⁶Sacrifice and offering You did not desire;
My ears you have opened;
Burnt offering and sin offering You did not require.
⁷Then I said, "Behold, I come;
In the scroll of the Book *it is* written of me.
⁸I delight to do Your will, O my God,
And Your law *is* within my heart."

⁹I have proclaimed the good news of righteousness
In the great congregation;
Indeed, I do not restrain my lips,
O LORD, You Yourself know.
¹⁰I have not hidden Your righteousness within my
    heart;
I have declared Your faithfulness and Your salvation;
I have not concealed Your lovingkindness and Your
    truth
From the great congregation.

Seek God's help against all evil.

¹¹Do not withhold Your tender mercies from me, O
    LORD;
Let Your lovingkindness and Your truth continually
    preserve me.
¹²For innumerable evils have surrounded me;
My iniquities have overtaken me, so that I am not
    able to look up;

They are more than the hairs of my head;
Therefore my heart fails me.

[13]Be pleased, O LORD, to deliver me;
O LORD, make haste to help me!
[14]Let them be ashamed and brought to mutual
confusion
Who seek to destroy my life;
Let them be driven backward and brought to
dishonor
Who wish me evil.
[15]Let them be appalled because of their shame,
Who say to me, "Aha, aha!"

Rest in the gladness and peace of God's saving and delivering grace.

[16]Let all those who seek You rejoice and be glad in
You;
Let such as love Your salvation say continually,
"The LORD be magnified!"
[17]But I *am* poor and needy;
Yet the LORD thinks upon me.
You *are* my help and my deliverer;
Do not delay, O my God.

Psalm 41

David, perhaps realizing that he has neglected the poor, is ill and oppressed by enemies and seeks the Lord's forgiveness and deliverance. Let this psalm provoke you to consider whether there are any good works you are neglecting. Read James 1:23–25; 4:17.

To the Chief Musician. A Psalm of David.

Have you neglected any good works? Remember that God blesses those who obey Him.

¹Blessed *is* he who considers the poor;
The LORD will deliver him in time of trouble.
²The LORD will preserve him and keep him alive,
And he will be blessed on the earth;
You will not deliver him to the will of his enemies.
³The LORD will strengthen him on his bed of illness;
You will sustain him on his sickbed.

Seek forgiveness for sins of omission.

⁴I said, "LORD, be merciful to me;
Heal my soul, for I have sinned against You."
⁵My enemies speak evil of me:
"When will he die, and his name perish?"
⁶And if he comes to see *me,* he speaks vain *words;*
His heart gathers iniquity to itself;
When he goes out, he tells *it.*

Seek God's deliverance from oppressors—whether human or spiritual.

⁷All who hate me whisper together against me;
Against me they devise my hurt.
⁸"An evil disease," *they say,* "clings to him.
And *now* that he lies down, he will rise up no more."
⁹Even my own familiar friend in whom I trusted,
Who ate my bread,
Has lifted up *his* heel against me.

¹⁰But You, O LORD, be merciful to me, and raise me
up,
That I may repay them.
¹¹By this I know that You are well pleased with me,
Because my enemy does not triumph over me.

¹²As for me, You uphold me in my integrity,
And set me before Your face forever.

¹³Blessed *be* the LORD God of Israel
From everlasting to everlasting!
Amen and Amen.

Psalm 42

Use this psalm of complaint to prepare your heart for times of trouble or despairing, or to intercede for those who are disturbed in their souls. Read 2 Corinthians 1:3–7.

To the Chief Musician. A Contemplation of the sons of Korah.

Pray that your soul may thirst for God.

¹As the deer pants for the water brooks,
So pants my soul for You, O God.
²My soul thirsts for God, for the living God.
When shall I come and appear before God?
³My tears have been my food day and night,
While they continually say to me,
"Where *is* your God?"

Recall the joy of being in God's presence in worship.

⁴When I remember these *things,*
I pour out my soul within me.
For I used to go with the multitude;
I went with them to the house of God,
With the voice of joy and praise,
With a multitude that kept a pilgrim feast.

Hope in God when your soul is cast down within you.

⁵Why are you cast down, O my soul?
And why are you disquieted within me?
Hope in God,
for I shall yet praise Him
For the help of His countenance.

Recall God's might when trouble rolls over you.

⁶O my God, my soul is cast down within me;
Therefore I will remember You from the land of the
    Jordan,
And from the heights of Hermon,
From the Hill Mizar.
⁷Deep calls unto deep at the noise of Your waterfalls;
All Your waves and billows have gone over me.
⁸The LORD will command His lovingkindness in the
    daytime,
And in the night His song *shall be* with me—
A prayer to the God of my life.

Resolve to seek the Lord and to praise Him in times of mourning or despair.

⁹I will say to God my Rock,
"Why have You forgotten me?
Why do I go mourning because of the oppression of
    the enemy?"
¹⁰*As* with a breaking of my bones,
My enemies reproach me,
While they say to me all day long,
"Where *is* your God?"

¹¹Why are you cast down, O my soul?
And why are you disquieted within me?
Hope in God;
For I shall yet praise Him,
The help of my countenance and my God.

Psalm 43

As in the previous psalm, in this psalm of complaint the psalmist finds peace and vindication in worshiping the Lord. Use it to keep things in perspective when trouble besets you. Read Acts 7:54–60.

Rest in God when troubles come.

¹Vindicate me, O God,
And plead my case against an ungodly nation;
Oh, deliver me from the deceitful and unjust man!
²For You *are* the God of my strength;
Why do You cast me off?
Why do I go mourning because of the oppression of
     the enemy?

Seek guidance from the Lord to lead you to worship Him.

³Oh, send out Your light and Your truth!
Let them lead me;
Let them bring me to Your holy hill
And to Your tabernacle.
⁴Then I will go to the altar of God,
To God my exceeding joy;
And on the harp I will praise You,
O God, my God.

Resolve to hope in God when you are despairing.

⁵Why are you cast down, O my soul?
And why are you disquieted within me?
Hope in God;
For I shall yet praise him,
The help of my countenance and my God.

Psalm 44

*This psalm combines elements of complaint and testimony
of God's kingly power to seek His grace for renewal. This is
an excellent psalm to use in calling upon the Lord to revive
His church. Read Revelation 3:1–6.*

To the Chief Musician. A Contemplation of the sons of Korah.

Recall the many times God has delivered and revived His church throughout the ages.

¹We have heard with our ears, O God,
Our fathers have told us,
What deeds You did in their days,
In days of old:
²*How* You drove out the nations with Your hand,
But them You planted;
How You afflicted the peoples, and cast them out.
³For they did not gain possession of the land by their
    own sword,
Nor did their own arm save them;
But it was Your right hand, Your arm, and the light of
    Your countenance,
Because You favored them.

Seek God's help to rise above the enemies of your soul.

⁴You are my King, O God;
Command victories for Jacob.
⁵Through You we will push down our enemies;
Through Your name we will trample those who rise
    up against us.
⁶For I will not trust in my bow,
Nor shall my sword save me.
⁷But You have saved us from our enemies,
And have put to shame those who hated us.

[8]In God we boast all day long,
And praise Your name forever.

Selah

Survey the condition of the church today, and pray for repentance and renewal.

[9]But You have cast *us* off and put us to shame,
And You do not go out with our armies.
[10]You make us turn back from the enemy,
And those who hate us have taken spoil for
    themselves.
[11]You have given us up like sheep *intended* for food,
And have scattered us among the nations.
[12]You sell Your people for naught,
And are not enriched by their price.

[13]You make us a reproach to our neighbors,
A scorn and a derision to those all around us.
[14]You make us a byword among the nations,
A shaking of the head among the peoples.
[15]My dishonor *is* continually before me,
And the shame of my face has covered me,
[16]Because of the voice of him who reproaches and
    reviles,
Because of the enemy and the avenger.

Confess your continuing trust in the Lord.

[17]All this has come upon us;
But we have not forgotten You,
Nor have we dealt falsely with Your covenant.

18Our heart has not turned back,
Nor have our steps departed from Your way;
19But You have severely broken us in the place of
    jackals,
And covered us with the shadow of death.

20If we had forgotten the name of our God,
Or stretched out our hands to a foreign god,
21Would not God search this out?
For He knows the secrets of the heart.
22Yet for Your sake we are killed all day long;
We are accounted as sheep for the slaughter.

Seek the Lord's grace for revival.

23Awake! Why do You sleep, O Lord?
Arise! Do not cast *us* off forever.
24Why do You hide Your face,
And forget our affliction and our oppression?
25For our soul is bowed down to the dust;
Our body clings to the ground.
26Arise for our help,
And redeem us for Your mercies' sake.

Psalm 45

This beautiful royal psalm celebrates the reign of King Jesus, seeks the progress of His kingdom, and glories in the wonders of His heavenly court. Use it to praise the Lord, work for the advance of His kingdom, and anticipate the blessings which are to come. Read Matthew 6:33; Revelation 21.

To the Chief Musician. Set to "The Lilies." A Contemplation of the sons of Korah. A Song of Love.

Praise Jesus our exalted King.

¹My heart is overflowing with a good theme;
I recite my composition concerning the King;
My tongue *is* the pen of a ready writer.
²You are fairer than the sons of men;
Grace is poured upon Your lips;
Therefore God has blessed You forever.

Pray that His kingdom might advance on earth, as in heaven.

³Gird Your sword upon *Your* thigh, O Mighty One,
With Your glory and Your majesty.
⁴And in Your majesty ride prosperously because of
    truth, humility, *and* righteousness;
And Your right hand shall teach You awesome things.
⁵Your arrows *are* sharp in the heart of the King's
    enemies;
The peoples fall under You.

Praise Christ in the glory of His heavenly realm.

⁶Your throne, O God, *is* forever and ever;
A scepter of righteousness *is* the scepter of Your
    kingdom.

[7]You love righteousness and hate wickedness;
Therefore God, Your God, has anointed You
With the oil of gladness more than Your companions.
[8]All Your garments *are scented* with myrrh and aloes
   and cassia,
Out of the ivory palaces, by which they have made
   You glad.
[9]Kings' daughters *are* among Your honorable women;
At Your right hand stands the queen in gold from
   Ophir.

Rededicate yourself to follow and worship Christ alone.

[10]Listen, O daughter,
Consider and incline your ear;
Forget your own people also, and your father's house;
[11]So the King will greatly desire your beauty;
Because He *is* your Lord, worship Him.
[12]And the daughter of Tyre *will be there* with a gift;
The rich among the people will seek your favor.

Meditate in praise on the glory that is to come.

[13]The royal daughter *is* all glorious within *the palace;*
Her clothing *is* woven with gold.
[14]She shall be brought to the King in robes of many
   colors;
The virgins, her companions who follow her, shall be
   brought to You.
[15]With gladness and rejoicing they shall be brought;
They shall enter the King's palace.

Seek the blessing of God for the generations to come; commit yourself to serving them.

[16]Instead of Your fathers shall be Your sons,
Whom You shall make princes in all the earth.

¹⁷I will make Your name to be remembered in all
    generations;
Therefore the people shall praise You forever and
    ever.

Psalm 46

*This powerful testimony psalm celebrates the mighty pres-
ence of God with His people. Use this psalm to renew confidence in Him in the face of trouble. Read Romans 8:31–39.*

To the Chief Musician. *A Psalm* of the sons of Korah. A Song for Alamoth.

**Praise the Lord, who protects us in the face of
every trial.**

¹God *is* our refuge and strength,
A very present help in trouble.
²Therefore we will not fear,
Though the earth be removed,
And though the mountains be carried into the midst
    of the sea;
³*Though* its waters roar and be troubled,
Though the mountains shake with its swelling.

Selah

**Rejoice in the river of God's grace, our constant
source of help.**

⁴*There is* a river whose streams shall make glad the
    city of God,
The holy *place* of the tabernacle of the Most High.

⁵God *is* in the midst of her, she shall not be moved;
God shall help her, just at the break of dawn.
⁶The nations raged, the kingdoms were moved;
He uttered His voice, the earth melted.

Praise the Lord for His constant presence.

⁷The LORD of hosts *is* with us;
The God of Jacob *is* our refuge.

Selah

Meditate on God's power, as seen in His mighty works.

⁸Come, behold the works of the LORD,
Who has made desolations in the earth.
⁹He makes wars to cease to the end of the earth;
He breaks the bow and cuts the spear in two;
He burns the chariot in the fire.

Rest in the mighty presence of God.

¹⁰Be still, and know that I *am* God;
I will be exalted among the nations,
I will be exalted in the earth!

¹¹The LORD of hosts *is* with us;
The God of Jacob *is* our refuge.

Selah

Psalm 47

This royal psalm celebrates the reign of God over the nations.
Use it to renew your commitment to the Great Commission.
Read Matthew 28:18–20.

To the Chief Musician. A Psalm of the sons of Korah.

Pray that the nations and peoples of the earth may come increasingly under God's rule and worship Him.

> ¹Oh, clap your hands, all you peoples!
> Shout to God with the voice of triumph!
> ²For the LORD Most High is awesome;
> *He is* a great King over all the earth.
> ³He will subdue the peoples under us,
> And the nations under our feet.
> ⁴He will choose our inheritance for us,
> The excellence of Jacob whom He loves.

> Selah

Rejoice in the exaltation of King Jesus, and celebrate His mighty rule.

> ⁵God has gone up with a shout,
> The LORD with the sound of a trumpet.
> ⁶Sing praises to God, sing praises!
> Sing praises to our King, sing praises!
> ⁷For God *is* the King of all the earth;
> Sing praises with understanding.

> ⁸God reigns over the nations;
> God sits on His holy throne.
> ⁹The princes of the people have gathered together,
> The people of the God of Abraham.
> For the shields of the earth *belong* to God;
> He is greatly exalted.

Psalm 48

This testimony psalm celebrates the glory of Zion—the church—and reflects on the goodness of God to His people. Use it to renew your vision for the church and to commit yourself to working for its edification. Read Hebrews 12:22–29.

A Song. A Psalm of the sons of Korah.

Ask God to give you a renewed vision of His church in its glory.

¹Great *is* the LORD, and greatly to be praised
In the city of our God,
In His holy mountain.
²Beautiful in elevation,
The joy of the whole earth,
Is Mount Zion *on* the sides of the north,
The city of the great King.
³God *is* in her palaces;
He is known as her refuge.

Pray that the rulers of the earth may be astounded at the glory of God in the church.

⁴For behold, the kings assembled,
They passed by together.
⁵They saw *it, and* so they marveled;
They were troubled, they hastened away.
⁶Fear took hold of them there,
And pain, as of a woman in travail,
⁷*As when* You break the ships of Tarshish
With an east wind.

⁸As we have heard,
So we have seen
In the city of the LORD of hosts,

In the city of our God:
God will establish it forever.

Selah

Recall the goodness of God to His church.

⁹We have thought, O God, on Your lovingkindness,
In the midst of Your temple.
¹⁰According to Your name, O God,
So *is* Your praise to the ends of the earth;
Your right hand is full of righteousness.
¹¹Let Mount Zion rejoice,
Let the daughters of Judah be glad,
Because of Your judgments.

Meditate on the glory of the church, and resolve to declare God's love to the generation to come.

¹²Walk about Zion,
And go all around her.
Count her towers;
¹³Mark well her bulwarks;
Consider her palaces;
That you may tell *it* to the generation following.
¹⁴For this *is* God,
Our God forever and ever;
He will be our guide
Even to death.

Psalm 49

This difficult wisdom psalm teaches us to rest in God's redeeming grace in the face of the prosperity of the wicked. Use this psalm to cultivate contentment in the midst of a prosperous but unbelieving generation. Read 1 Timothy 6:6–16.

To the Chief Musician. A Psalm of the sons of Korah.

Listen to the Lord as He prepares your heart to receive wisdom from His mouth.

¹Hear this, all *you* peoples;
Give ear, all *you* inhabitants of the world,
²Both low and high,
Rich and poor together.
³My mouth shall speak wisdom,
And the meditation of my heart *shall bring*
     understanding.
⁴I will incline my ear to a proverb;
I will disclose my dark saying on the harp.

Pray for those blinded by prosperity, that they will realize that redemption is not found in riches.

⁵Why should I fear in the days of evil,
When the iniquity at my heels surrounds me?
⁶Those who trust in their wealth
And boast in the multitude of their riches,
⁷None *of them* can by any means redeem *his* brother,
Nor give to God a ransom for him—
⁸For the redemption of their souls *is* costly,
And it shall cease forever—
⁹That he should continue to live eternally,
And not see the Pit.

Pray that God will bring the wicked to see the foolishness of their ways.

¹⁰For he sees *that* wise men die;
Likewise the fool and the senseless person perish,
And leave their wealth to others.

[11]Their inner thought is *that* their houses *will continue* forever,
And their dwelling places to all generations;
They call *their* lands after their own names.
[12]Nevertheless man, *though* in honor, does not remain;
He is like the beasts *that* perish.

[13]This is the way of those who *are* foolish,
And of their posterity who approve their sayings.

Selah

[14]Like sheep they are laid in the grave;
Death shall feed on them;
The upright shall have dominion over them in the morning;
And their beauty shall be consumed in the grave, far from their dwelling.

Praise God for the redemption we have in Christ.

[15]But God will redeem my soul from the power of the grave,
For He shall receive me.

Selah

Be content in God's gracious care, and pray for the lost.

[16]Do not be afraid when one becomes rich,
When the glory of his house is increased;
[17]For when he dies he shall carry nothing away;
His glory shall not descend after him.
[18]Though while he lives he blesses himself
(For *men* will praise you when you do well for yourself),
[19]He shall go to the generation of his fathers;
They shall never see light.

²⁰Man *who* is in honor, yet does not understand,
Is like the beasts *that* perish.

Psalm 50

*In this psalm of admonition Asaph advises the people of God
to scrutinize their worship of Him. This psalm can help us
to examine our own worship and to pray for those whose
worship is merely superficial. Read Romans 14:14–20;
1 Corinthians 4:20.*

A Psalm of Asaph.

Pray for a renewed vision of God in His greatness and might.

¹The Mighty One, God the LORD,
Has spoken and called the earth
From the rising of the sun to its going down.
²Out of Zion, the perfection of beauty,
God will shine forth.
³Our God shall come, and shall not keep silent;
A fire shall devour before Him,
And it shall be very tempestuous all around Him.

⁴He shall call to the heavens from above,
And to the earth, that He may judge His people:
⁵"Gather My saints together to Me,
Those who have made a covenant with Me by
	sacrifice."
⁶Let the heavens declare His righteousness,
For God Himself *is* Judge.

Selah

Review your own worship: Is it merely outward or truly from the heart?

> [7]"Hear, O My people, and I will speak,
> O Israel, and I will testify against you;
> I *am* God, your God!
> [8]I will not reprove you for your sacrifices
> Or your burnt offerings,
> *Which are* continually before Me.
> [9]I will not take a bull from your house,
> *Nor* goats out of your folds.
> [10]For every beast of the forest *is* Mine,
> *And* the cattle on a thousand hills.
> [11]I know all the birds of the mountains,
> And the wild beasts of the field *are* Mine.
>
> [12]"If I were hungry, I would not tell you;
> For the world is Mine, and all its fullness.
> [13]Will I eat the flesh of bulls,
> Or drink the blood of goats?
> [14]Offer to God thanksgiving,
> And pay your vows to the Most High.
> [15]Call upon Me in the day of trouble;
> I will deliver you, and you shall glorify Me."

Pray for all who worship God insincerely or without truly knowing and obeying Him.

> [16]But to the wicked God says:
> "What *right* have you to declare My statutes,
> Or take My covenant in your mouth,
> [17]Seeing you hate instruction
> And cast My words behind you?
> [18]When you saw a thief, you consented with him,
> And have been a partaker with adulterers.
> [19]You give your mouth to evil,
> And your tongue frames deceit.

²⁰You sit *and* speak against your brother;
You slander your own mother's son.
²¹These *things* you have done, and I kept silent;
You thought that I was altogether like you;
But I will reprove you,
And set *them* in order before your eyes.

Resolve to worship God from the heart, in Spirit and in truth.

²²"Now consider this, you who forget God,
Lest I tear *you* in pieces,
And *there* be none to deliver:
²³Whoever offers praise glorifies Me;
And to him who orders *his* conduct *aright*
I will show the salvation of God."

Psalm 51

Here is the classic psalm of confession, useful for setting our accounts straight with the Lord and for seeking His help against temptation day by day. Read 1 John 1:8–9.

To the Chief Musician. A Psalm of David when Nathan the prophet went to him, after he had gone in to Bathsheba.

Thank God for His mercy, that in Jesus Christ we have forgiveness of our sins.

¹Have mercy upon me, O God,
According to Your lovingkindness;
According to the multitude of Your tender mercies,
Blot out my transgressions.
²Wash me thoroughly from my iniquity,
And cleanse me from my sin.

Acknowledge specific sins to God as His Spirit leads.

³For I acknowledge my transgressions,
And my sin *is* ever before me.
⁴Against You, You only, have I sinned,
And done *this* evil in Your sight—
That You may be found just when You speak,
And blameless when You judge.

Recall God's desires for you, and thank Him for the cleansing blood of Christ.

⁵Behold, I was brought forth in iniquity,
And in sin my mother conceived me.
⁶Behold, You desire truth in the inward parts,
And in the hidden *part* You will make me to know
    wisdom.

⁷Purge me with hyssop, and I shall be clean;
Wash me, and I shall be whiter than snow.
⁸Make me to hear joy and gladness,
That the bones *which* You have broken may rejoice.
⁹Hide Your face from my sins,
And blot out all my iniquities.

Seek cleansing and renewal in God's Spirit.

¹⁰Create in me a clean heart, O God,
And renew a steadfast spirit within me.
¹¹Do not cast me away from Your presence,
And do not take Your Holy Spirit from me.

¹²Restore to me the joy of Your salvation,
And uphold me *with Your* generous Spirit.
¹³*Then* I will teach transgressors Your ways,
And sinners will be converted to You.

Let God break your sinful bent and lead you to praise Him more and more.

¹⁴Deliver me from bloodguiltiness, O God,
The God of my salvation,
And my tongue shall sing aloud of Your
 righteousness.
¹⁵O Lord, open my lips,
And my mouth shall show forth Your praise.
¹⁶For You do not desire sacrifice, or else I would give
 it;
You do not delight in burnt offering.
¹⁷The sacrifices of God *are* a broken spirit,
A broken and a contrite heart—
These, O God, You will not despise.

Be renewed for the building up of the church.

¹⁸Do good in Your good pleasure to Zion;
Build the walls of Jerusalem.
¹⁹Then You shall be pleased with the sacrifices of
 righteousness,
With burnt offering and whole burnt offering;
Then they shall offer bulls on Your altar.

Psalm 52

This psalm combines elements of imprecation and wisdom to lead us to wait on the Lord in the midst of an unbelieving generation. Read Philippians 2:12–16.

To the Chief Musician. A Contemplation of David when Doeg the Edomite went and told Saul, and said to him, "David has gone to the house of Ahimelech."

Deplore the ingratitude and sinfulness of the wicked, and allow God to search your own soul.

¹Why do you boast in evil, O mighty man?
The goodness of God *endures* continually.
²Your tongue devises destruction,
Like a sharp razor, working deceitfully.
³You love evil more than good,
And lying rather than speaking righteousness.

Selah

⁴You love all devouring words,
You deceitful tongue.

Trust God to deal with the wicked.

⁵God shall likewise destroy you forever;
He shall take you away, and pluck you out of *your*
  dwelling place,
And uproot you from the land of the living.

Selah

⁶The righteous also shall see and fear,
And shall laugh at him, *saying,*
⁷"Here is the man who did not make God his
  strength,
But trusted in the abundance of his riches,
And strengthened himself in his wickedness."

Rest in the mercy of God, and seek grace to live fruitfully for Him.

⁸But I *am* like a green olive tree in the house of God;
I trust in the mercy of God forever and ever.
⁹I will praise You forever,
Because You have done *it;*
And in the presence of Your saints
I will wait on Your name, for *it is* good.

Psalm 53

This psalm of complaint repeats themes evoked in Psalm 14, but with a little twist just before the end. Trust God to deal justly with the wicked, and call on Him to renew His people. Read Matthew 5:11–16.

To the Chief Musician. Set to "Mahalath." A Contemplation of David.

Pray for the lost, who deny the Lord and follow wicked ways.

¹The fool has said in his heart,
"*There* is no God."
They are corrupt, and have done abominable
        iniquity;
There is none who does good.

²God looks down from heaven upon the children of
        men,
To see if there are *any* who understand, who seek
        God.
³Every one of them has turned aside;
They have together become corrupt;

There is none who does good,
No, not one.

Pray for God's people who are persecuted by the wicked.

⁴Have the workers of iniquity no knowledge,
Who eat up my people as they eat bread,
And do not call upon God?
⁵There they are in great fear
Where no fear was,
For God has scattered the bones of him who
    encamps against you;
You have put *them* to shame,
Because God has despised them.

Pray for renewal in the church.

⁶Oh, that the salvation of Israel would come out of
    Zion!
When God brings back the captivity of His people,
Let Jacob rejoice *and* Israel be glad.

Psalm 54

In this psalm of complaint and testimony, David renews his trust in the Lord in the face of adversity. We can use it to seek God's help against our foes, be they human or spiritual. Read Ephesians 6:10–20.

To the Chief Musician. With stringed instruments. A Contemplation of David when the
Ziphites went and said to Saul, "Is David not hiding with us?"

**Rest in the Lord to vindicate and protect you
against the accusations and threats of all foes.**

¹Save me, O God, by Your name,
And vindicate me by Your strength.
²Hear my prayer, O God;
Give ear to the words of my mouth.
³For strangers have risen up against me,
And oppressors have sought after my life;
They have not set God before them.

Selah

**Express your confidence in the Lord, and praise
His name.**

⁴Behold, God *is* my helper;
The Lord *is* with those who uphold my life.
⁵He will repay my enemies for their evil.
Cut them off in Your truth.

⁶I will freely sacrifice to You;
I will praise Your name, O LORD, for *it is* good.
⁷For He has delivered me out of all trouble;
And my eye has seen *its desire* upon my enemies.

Psalm 55

In this psalm of complaint, David, perplexed and saddened by betrayal, resolves to cast his burden on the Lord to sustain and care for him. Whatever our trials, we can cast them on the Lord, and He will bear them. Read Philippians 4:6–7; 1 Peter 5:6–7.

To the Chief Musician. With stringed instruments. A Contemplation of David.

Call upon God to hear you in your trouble.

¹Give ear to my prayer, O God,
And do not hide Yourself from my supplication.
²Attend to me, and hear me;
I am restless in my complaint, and moan noisily,
³Because of the voice of the enemy,
Because of the oppression of the wicked;
For they bring down trouble upon me,
And in wrath they hate me.

Express your deep feelings to the Lord.

⁴My heart is severely pained within me,
And the terrors of death have fallen upon me.
⁵Fearfulness and trembling have come upon me,
And horror has overwhelmed me.
⁶And I said, "Oh, that I had wings like a dove!
For then I would fly away and be at rest.
⁷Indeed, I would wander far off,
And remain in the wilderness.

Selah

⁸I would hasten my escape
From the windy storm *and* tempest."

Call upon God to deal with your enemies, or those of His people.

⁹Destroy, O Lord, *and* divide their tongues,
For I have seen violence and strife in the city.
¹⁰Day and night they go around it on its walls;
Iniquity and trouble *are* also in the midst of it.
¹¹Destruction *is* in its midst;
Deceit and guile do not depart from its streets.

Express your specific concern, or that of those who suffer, to the Lord. Recall the suffering of Christ, who was betrayed.

¹²For it is not an enemy *who* reproaches me;
Then I could bear *it.*
Nor *is it* one *who* hates me who has magnified *himself*
  against me;
Then I could hide from him.
¹³But *it was* you, a man my equal,
My companion and my acquaintance.
¹⁴We took sweet counsel together,
And walked to the house of God in the throng.

¹⁵Let death seize them;
Let them go down alive into hell,
For wickedness *is* in their dwellings *and* among them.

Resolve to wait on the Lord in prayer.

¹⁶As for me, I will call upon God,
And the Lᴏʀᴅ shall save me.
¹⁷Evening and morning and at noon
I will pray, and cry aloud,
And He shall hear my voice.
¹⁸He has redeemed my soul in peace from the battle
  which was against me, for there were many against
  me.

[19]God will hear, and afflict them,
Even He who abides from of old.

Selah

Because they do not change,
Therefore they do not fear God.

[20]He has put forth his hands against those who were
   at peace with him;
He has broken his covenant.
[21]*The words* of his mouth were smoother than butter,
But war was in his heart;
His words were softer than oil,
Yet they *were* drawn swords.

[22]Cast your burden on the LORD,
And He shall sustain you;
He shall never permit the righteous to be moved.

Thank God for His justice and mercy.

[23]But You, O God, shall bring them down to the pit of
   destruction;
Bloodthirsty and deceitful men shall not live out half
   their days;
But I will trust in You.

Psalm 56

In this psalm of complaint David seeks protection and deliverance from his enemies. As you pray this, think of the persecuted church, or the temptations and trials you will face this day, and call upon the Lord for help. Read John 16:33.

To the Chief Musician. Set to "The Silent Dove in Distant Lands." A Michtam of David when the Philistines captured him in Gath.

Resolve to trust in God in the face of every fear or trial.

¹Be merciful to me, O God, for man would swallow
  me up;
Fighting all day he oppresses me.
²My enemies would hound me all day,
For *there are* many who fight against me, O Most
  High.

³Whenever I am afraid,
I will trust in You.
⁴In God (I will praise His word),
In God I have put my trust;
I will not fear.
What can flesh do to me?

Set your specific complaints or concerns before the Lord.

⁵All day they twist my words;
All their thoughts *are* against me for evil.
⁶They gather together,
They hide, they mark my steps,
When they lie in wait for my life.
⁷Shall they escape by iniquity?
In anger cast down the peoples, O God!

Seek God's compassion and help against all your enemies.

⁸You number my wanderings;
Put my tears into Your bottle;
Are they not in Your book?
⁹When I cry out *to You,*
Then my enemies will turn back;
This I know, because God *is* for me.

[10]In God (I will praise *His* word),
In the LORD (I will praise *His* word),
[11]In God I have put my trust;
I will not be afraid.
What can man do to me?

Renew your vows and commitment to the Lord.

[12]Vows *made* to You *are binding* upon me, O God;
I will render praises to You,
[13]For You have delivered my soul from death.
Have You not *delivered* my feet from falling,
That I may walk before God
In the light of the living?

Psalm 57

This is a psalm of complaint and testimony, in which David declares his trust in the Lord in the face of adversity. As with the previous psalm, use this one to intercede for the persecuted church, to seek God's help in your own trials, or to prepare you for the temptations you will face each day. Read Matthew 7:7–14.

To the Chief Musician. Set to "Do Not Destroy." A Michtam of David when he fled from Saul into the cave.

Seek God's mercy and deliverance in the face of adversity or trial.

[1]Be merciful to me, O God, be merciful to me!
For my soul trusts in You;
And in the shadow of Your wings I will make my
    refuge,
Until *these* calamities have passed by.

[2]I will cry out to God Most High,
To God who performs *all things* for me.
[3]He shall send from heaven and save me;
He reproaches the one who would swallow me up.

Selah

God shall send forth His mercy and His truth.

Bring your particular complaint or concerns before the Lord, and exalt Him.

[4]My soul is among lions;
I lie *among* the sons of men
Who are set on fire,
Whose teeth *are* spears and arrows,
And their tongue a sharp sword.
[5]Be exalted, O God, above the heavens;
Let Your glory *be* above all the earth.

[6]They have prepared a net for my steps;
My soul is bowed down;
They have dug a pit before me;
Into the midst of it they *themselves* have fallen.

Selah

Declare your trust in the Lord, and resolve to praise Him more and more.

[7]My heart is steadfast, O God, my heart is steadfast;
I will sing and give praise.
[8]Awake, my glory!
Awake, lute and harp!
I will awaken the dawn.

[9]I will praise You, O Lord, among the peoples;
I will sing to You among the nations.
[10]For Your mercy reaches unto the heavens,
And Your truth unto the clouds.

Exalt the Lord, and praise His name!

[11]Be exalted, O God, above the heavens;
Let Your glory *be* above all the earth.

Psalm 58

This psalm combines aspects of complaint, admonition, and imprecation to seek the justice of God against His enemies. Use it to pray that those who oppose the Lord may come to their senses and seek Him before they fall under His wrath. Read Acts 17:26–31; Romans 1:18–32.

To the Chief Musician. Set to "Do Not Destroy." A Michtam of David.

Meditate on the wickedness of those who do not seek the way of the Lord.

[1]Do you indeed speak righteousness, you silent ones?
Do you judge uprightly, you sons of men?
[2]No, in heart you work wickedness;
You weigh out the violence of your hands in the earth.

Consider the desperate situation of the wicked, and call on God to humble and break them.

[3]The wicked are estranged from the womb;
They go astray as soon as they are born, speaking lies.
[4]Their poison *is* like the poison of a serpent;
They are like the deaf cobra *that* stops its ear,
[5]Which will not heed the voice of charmers,
Charming ever so skillfully.

[6]Break their teeth in their mouth, O God!
Break out the fangs of the young lions, O LORD!

⁷Let them flow away as waters *which* run continually;
When he bends *his bow,*
Let his arrows be as if cut in pieces.
⁸*Let them be* like a snail which melts away as it goes,
Like a stillborn child of a woman, that they may not
see the sun.

**Praise the Lord, and call upon Him to be glorified
in rendering justice against His foes.**

⁹Before your pots can feel *the burning* thorns,
He shall take them away as with a whirlwind,
As in His living and burning wrath.
¹⁰The righteous shall rejoice when he sees the
vengeance;
He shall wash his feet in the blood of the wicked,
¹¹So that men will say,
"Surely *there* is a reward for the righteous;
Surely He is God who judges in the earth."

Psalm 59

*David complains to God about his enemies and resolves to
trust in His saving power. We can pray this psalm as the previous three, seeking God's help in the face of adversity, trial,
and temptation. Read 2 Timothy 3:10–17.*

To the Chief Musician. Set to "Do Not Destroy." A Michtam of David when Saul sent
men, and they watched the house in order to kill him.

**Cry to God for deliverance from the specific trials
you are facing.**

¹Deliver me from my enemies, O my God;
Defend me from those who rise up against me.

²Deliver me from the workers of iniquity,
And save me from bloodthirsty men.

³For look, they lie in wait for my life;
The mighty gather against me,
Not *for* my transgressions nor *for* my sin, O LORD.
⁴They run and prepare themselves through no fault of
    mine.

Call upon the Lord to deal with your foes and His.

Awake to help me, and behold!
⁵You therefore, O LORD God of hosts, the God of
    Israel,
Awake to punish all the nations;
Do not be merciful to any wicked transgressors.

                                      Selah

⁶At evening they return,
They growl like a dog,
And go all around the city.
⁷Indeed, they belch out with their mouth;
Swords *are* in their lips;
For *they say,* "Who hears?"

⁸But You, O LORD, shall laugh at them;
You shall have all the nations in derision.
⁹*O You* his Strength,
I will wait for you.

For God *is* my defense;
¹⁰My merciful God shall come to meet me;
God shall let me see *my desire* on my enemies.

Pray that God would make His judgment and Himself known to His enemies.

[11]Do not slay them, lest my people forget;
Scatter them by Your power,
And bring them down,
O Lord our shield.
[12]*For* the sin of their mouth *and* the words of their
    lips,
Let them even be taken in their pride,
And for the cursing and lying *which* they speak.
[13]Consume *them* in wrath, consume *them,*
That they *may* not *be;*
And let them know that God rules in Jacob
To the ends of the earth.

Selah

Sing praise to God, and rest in His power in the face of all adversity and every foe.

[14]And at evening they return,
They growl like a dog,
And go all around the city.
[15]They wander up and down for food,
And howl if they are not satisfied.

[16]But I will sing of Your power;
Yes, I will sing aloud of Your mercy in the morning;
For You have been my defense
And refuge in the day of my trouble.
[17]To You, O my Strength, I will sing praises;
For God *is* my defense,
The God of my mercy.

Psalm 60

In this psalm of complaint and testimony, David calls upon the Lord to renew Israel in her mission and calling. Use it to seek revival and renewal in the church of our Lord Jesus. Read Revelation 3:14–22.

To the Chief Musician. Set to "Lily of the Testimony." A Michtam of David. For teaching. When he fought against Mesopotamia and Syria of Zobah, and Joab returned and killed twelve thousand Edomites in the Valley of Salt.

Consider the state of the church and its need for God's reviving grace.

¹O God, You have cast us off;
You have broken us down;
You have been displeased;
Oh, restore us again!
²You have made the earth tremble;
You have broken it;
Heal its breaches, for it is shaking.
³You have shown Your people hard things;
You have made us drink the wine of confusion.

Recall the church's mission of declaring the love of Christ, and claim God's promise to bring in the nations.

⁴You have given a banner to those who fear You,
That it may be displayed because of the truth.

Selah

⁵That Your beloved may be delivered,
Save *with* Your right hand, and hear me.

[6]God has spoken in His holiness:
"I will rejoice;
I will divide Shechem
And measure out the Valley of Succoth.
[7]Gilead *is* Mine, and Manasseh *is* Mine;
Ephraim also *is* the helmet for My head;
Judah *is* My lawgiver.
[8]Moab *is* My washpot;
Over Edom I will cast My shoe;
Philistia, shout in triumph because of Me."

Cry out to God to renew His church.

[9]Who will bring me *into* the strong city?
Who will lead me to Edom?
[10]*Is it* not You, O God, *who* cast us off?
And *You,* O God, *who* did not go out with our armies?
[11]Give us help from trouble,
For vain *is* the help of man.
[12]Through God we will do valiantly,
For *it is* He *who* shall tread down our enemies.

Psalm 61

David offers this psalm of testimony as a way of renewing his vows to the Lord. We may use it in just the same way, as we recommit ourselves to those relationships, roles, and responsibilities we have undertaken before the Lord. Read Galatians 6:1–10.

To the Chief Musician. On a stringed instrument. *A Psalm* of David.

Seek the Lord, that He might hear your prayer and give peace to your heart.

> ¹Hear my cry, O God;
> Attend to my prayer.
> ²From the end of the earth I will cry to You,
> When my heart is overwhelmed;
> Lead me to the rock that is higher than I.

Praise God for His faithful protection and care; renew your trust in Him.

> ³For You have been a shelter for me,
> *And* a strong tower from the enemy.
> ⁴I will abide in Your tabernacle forever;
> I will trust in the shelter of Your wings.

> Selah

Renew the vows and commitments you have made before the Lord.

> ⁵For You, O God, have heard my vows;
> You have given *me* the heritage of those who fear
>   Your name.
> ⁶You will prolong the king's life,
> His years as many generations.

⁷He shall abide before God forever,
Oh, prepare mercy and truth, *which* may preserve
  him!

⁸So I will sing praise to Your name forever,
That I may daily perform my vows.

Psalm 62

*This psalm contains elements of complaint and testimony,
as David resolves to wait on the Lord in the presence of some
unknown adversity. David's advice to "pour out your heart"
to the Lord should encourage us to be completely honest
before the Lord about our fears, needs, and deepest concerns.
Read Hebrews 4:14–16.*

To the Chief Musician. To Jeduthun. A Psalm of David.

Praise God for His care and protection; resolve to wait on Him in prayer.

¹Truly my soul silently *waits* for God;
From Him *comes* my salvation.
²He only *is* my rock and my salvation;
He is my defense;
I shall not be greatly moved.

Bring your concerns, trials, and fears to the Lord.

³How long will you attack a man?
You shall be slain, all of you,
Like a leaning wall and a tottering fence.
⁴They only consult to cast *him* down from his high
  position;

They delight in lies;
They bless with their mouth,
But they curse inwardly.

Selah

Praise the Lord who saves, defends, and strengthens you; wait on Him.

⁵My soul, wait silently for God alone,
For my expectation *is* from Him.
⁶He only is my rock and my salvation;
He is my defense;
I shall not be moved.
⁷In God *is* my salvation and my glory;
The rock of my strength,
And my refuge, *is* in God.

Bare your heart before the Lord, and trust wholly in Him.

⁸Trust in Him at all times, you people;
Pour out your heart before Him;
God *is* a refuge for us.

Selah

Renounce all other confidences.

⁹Surely men of low degree *are* a vapor,
Men of high degree *are* a lie;
If they are weighed in the balances,
They *are* altogether *lighter* than vapor.
¹⁰Do not trust in oppression,
Nor vainly hope in robbery;
If riches increase,
Do not set *your* heart *on them.*

Declare your trust in God alone, and seek His mercy for your needs.

> [11]God has spoken once,
> Twice I have heard this:
> That power *belongs* to God.
> [12]Also to you, O Lord, *belongs* mercy;
> For You render to each one according to his work.

Psalm 63

*In this psalm of testimony and praise David declares his con-
fidence in the Lord and resolves to seek Him earnestly. Use
this psalm to renew your trust in the Lord and your determination to live for Him. Read Colossians 1:9–12.*

A Psalm of David when he was in the wilderness of Judah.

Ask the Lord to increase your soul's desire for Him and to show you His glory.

> [1]O God, You *are* my God;
> Early will I seek You;
> My soul thirsts for You;
> My flesh longs for You
> In a dry and thirsty land
> Where there is no water.
> [2]So I have looked for You in the sanctuary,
> To see your power and Your glory.

Praise God for His many lovingkindnesses.

> [3]Because Your lovingkindness *is* better than life,
> My lips shall praise You.

⁴Thus will I bless You while I live;
I will lift up my hands in Your name.
⁵My soul shall be satisfied as with marrow and
    fatness,
And my mouth shall praise *You* with joyful lips.

Rejoice in the Lord's constant care.

⁶When I remember You on my bed,
I meditate on You in the *night* watches.
⁷Because You have been my help,
Therefore in the shadow of Your wings I will rejoice.
⁸My soul follows close behind You;
Your right hand upholds me.

Rest your fears and trials on the Lord.

⁹But those *who* seek my life, to destroy *it,*
Shall go into the lower parts of the earth.
¹⁰They shall fall by the sword;
They shall be a portion for jackals.

¹¹But the king shall rejoice in God;
Everyone who swears by Him shall glory;
But the mouth of those who speak lies shall be
    stopped.

Psalm 64

*In this psalm of complaint and imprecation, David calls on
the Lord to judge his enemies and resolves to rejoice in Him.
Use it to turn your cares over to the Lord and to renew your
hope in Him. Read Romans 12:19–21.*

To the Chief Musician. A Psalm of David.

Seek God's grace to calm your fears and to protect you from all foes.

¹Hear my voice, O God, in my meditation;
Preserve my life from fear of the enemy.
²Hide me from the secret counsel of the wicked,
From the insurrection of the workers of iniquity,
³Who sharpen their tongue like a sword,
And bend *their bows to shoot* their arrows—bitter
    words,
⁴That they may shoot in secret at the blameless;
Suddenly they shoot at him and do not fear.

Ask the Lord to see the plots of your enemies—human or spiritual—and to judge them to His praise and honor.

⁵They encourage themselves *in* an evil matter;
They talk of laying snares secretly;
They say, "Who will see them?"
⁶They devise iniquities:
"We have perfected a shrewd scheme."
Both the inward thought and the heart of man are
    deep.

⁷But God shall shoot at them *with* an arrow;
Suddenly they shall be wounded.
⁸So He will make them stumble over their own
    tongue;
All who see them shall flee away.
⁹All men shall fear,
And shall declare the work of God;
For they shall wisely consider His doing.

Rejoice in the Lord and His care for you.

¹⁰The righteous shall be glad in the LORD, and trust in
  Him.
And all the upright in heart shall glory.

Psalm 65

*This is a psalm of praise to God for His many wondrous
works. It can be used in just that way. Read Revelation
4:9–11.*

To the Chief Musician. A Psalm of David. A Song.

Praise the Lord, who forgives your sin.

¹Praise is awaiting You, O God, in Zion;
And to You the vow shall be performed.
²O You who hear prayer,
To You all flesh will come.
³Iniquities prevail against me;
As for our transgressions,
You will provide atonement for them.

**Praise the Lord for His having chosen and saved
you.**

⁴Blessed *is the man whom* You choose,
And cause to approach *You,*
That he may dwell in Your courts.
We shall be satisfied with the goodness of Your
  house,
Of Your holy temple.

Praise the Lord for His sovereign rule over all He has made.

> [5]*By* awesome deeds in righteousness You will answer us,
> O God of our salvation,
> *You who are* the confidence of all the ends of the earth,
> And of the far-off seas;
> [6]Who established the mountains by His strength,
> *Being* clothed with power;
> [7]You who still the noise of the seas,
> The noise of their waves,
> And the tumult of the peoples.
> [8]They also who dwell in the farthest parts are afraid of Your signs;
> You make the outgoings of the morning and evening rejoice.

Praise the Lord for His many works of providential care.

> [9]You visit the earth and water it,
> You greatly enrich it;
> The river of God is full of water;
> You provide their grain,
> For so You have prepared it.
> [10]You water its ridges abundantly,
> You settle its furrows;
> You make it soft with showers,
> You bless its growth.
>
> [11]You crown the year with Your goodness,
> And Your paths drip *with* abundance.
> [12]They drop *on* the pastures of the wilderness,
> And the little hills rejoice on every side.

¹³The pastures are clothed with flocks;
The valleys also are covered with grain;
They shout for joy, they also sing.

Psalm 66

The psalmist, having been brought through some adversity to a better place, offers praise to God and declares his firm faith in Him. This psalm can be most helpful in enabling us to keep our trials and sufferings in a proper perspective. Read Hebrews 12:3–11.

To the Chief Musician. A Song. A Psalm.

Celebrate the awesome works of God in praise to Him.

¹Make a joyful shout to God, all the earth!
²Sing out the honor of His name;
Make His praise glorious.
³Say to God,
"How awesome are Your works!
Through the greatness of Your power
Your enemies shall submit themselves to You.
⁴All the earth shall worship You
And sing praises to You;
They shall sing praises *to* Your name."

Selah

Review the many wondrous works of God, and consider your own trials within that context.

⁵Come and see the works of God;
He is awesome *in His* doing toward the sons of men.

⁶He turned the sea into dry *land;*
They went through the river on foot.
There we will rejoice in Him.
⁷He rules by His power forever;
His eyes observe the nations;
Do not let the rebellious exalt themselves.

Selah

⁸Oh, bless our God, you peoples!
And make the voice of His praise to be heard,
⁹Who keeps our soul among the living,
And does not allow our feet to be moved.
¹⁰For You, O God, have proved us;
You have refined us as silver is refined.
¹¹You brought us into the net;
You laid affliction on our backs.
¹²You have caused men to ride over our heads;
We went through fire and through water;
But You brought us out to rich *fulfillment.*

Renew your vows to the Lord, and prepare sacrifices of thanksgiving.

¹³I will go into Your house with burnt offerings;
I will pay You my vows,
¹⁴Which my lips have uttered
And my tongue has spoken when I was in trouble.
¹⁵I will offer You burnt sacrifices of fat animals,
With the sweet aroma of rams; I will offer bulls with
    goats.

Selah

Resolve to declare your faith in the Lord; search your heart for any lingering sin.

¹⁶Come *and* hear, all you who fear God,
And I will declare what He has done for my soul.
¹⁷I cried to Him with my mouth,
And He was extolled with my tongue.

[18]If I regard iniquity in my heart,
The Lord will not hear.
[19]*But* certainly God has heard *me;*
He has attended to the voice of my prayer.

[20]Blessed *be* God,
Who has not turned away my prayer,
Nor His mercy from me!

Psalm 67

*In the midst of God's many blessings, the psalmist longs for
the nations to fear the Lord. This is an excellent psalm to use
in considering the church's calling to invest its many blessings to reach the world for Christ. Read 3 John 5–8.*

To the Chief Musician. On stringed instruments. A Psalm. A Song.

**Seek the favor of God that you may be used of
Him to reach others for Christ.**

[1]God be merciful to us and bless us,
And cause His face to shine upon us.

Selah

[2]That Your way may be known on earth,
Your salvation among all nations.

**Name various individuals or peoples you or your
church are actively seeking to reach.**

[3]Let the peoples praise You, O God;
Let all the peoples praise You.
[4]Oh, let the nations be glad and sing for joy!
For You shall judge the people righteously,
And govern the nations on earth.

Selah

5Let the peoples praise You, O God;
Let all the peoples praise You.

Consecrate the blessings of God to the work of reaching the nations.

6*Then* the earth shall yield her increase;
God, our own God, shall bless us.
7God shall bless us,
And all the ends of the earth shall fear Him.

Psalm 68

This early psalm of David consists of many different aspects—praise, testimony, even imprecation. I find this psalm most useful in reviewing the grand scope of God's redemption in order to praise Him more gloriously and live for Him more completely. Read Colossians 3:1–14.

To the Chief Musician. A Psalm of David. A Song.

Pray that God may be exalted and His enemies scattered.

1Let God arise,
Let His enemies be scattered;
Let those who hate Him flee before Him.
2As smoke is driven away,
So drive *them* away;
As wax melts before the fire,
So let the wicked perish at the presence of God.
3But let the righteous be glad;
Let them rejoice before God;
Yes, let them rejoice exceedingly.

Review God's mercy to Israel, and praise Him for His salvation as we have come to know it in Christ.

⁴Sing to God, sing praises to His name;
Extol Him who rides on the clouds,
By His name YAH,
And rejoice before Him.

⁵A father of the fatherless, a defender of widows,
Is God in His holy habitation.
⁶God sets the solitary in families;
He brings out those who are bound into prosperity;
But the rebellious dwell in a dry *land.*

⁷O God, when You went out before Your people,
When You marched through the wilderness,

Selah

⁸The earth shook;
The heavens also dropped *rain* at the presence of
    God;
Sinai itself *was moved* at the presence of God, the God
    of Israel.
⁹You, O God, sent a plentiful rain,
Whereby You confirmed Your inheritance,
When it was weary.
¹⁰Your congregation dwelt in it;
You, O God, provided from Your goodness for the
    poor.

¹¹The Lord gave the word;
Great *was* the company of those who proclaimed *it:*
¹²"Kings of armies flee, they flee,
And she who remains at home divides the spoil.

¹³Though You lie down among the sheepfolds,
Yet you will be like the wings of a dove covered with
     silver,
And her feathers with yellow gold."
¹⁴When the Almighty scattered kings in it,
It was *white* as snow in Zalmon.

**Praise God for the diversity, richness, and vast
scope of His gifts and people.**

¹⁵A mountain of God *is* the mountain of Bashan;
A mountain *of many* peaks *is* the mountain of Bashan.
¹⁶Why do you fume with envy, you mountains of
     many peaks?
This is the mountain *which* God desires to dwell in;
Yes, the LORD will dwell *in it* forever.

¹⁷The chariots of God *are* twenty thousand,
Even thousands of thousands;
The Lord is among them *as in* Sinai, in the Holy
     Place.
¹⁸You have ascended on high,
You have led captivity captive;
You have received gifts among men,
Even *among* the rebellious,
That the LORD God might dwell *there.*

¹⁹Blessed *be* the Lord,
Who daily loads us *with benefits,*
The God of our salvation!

                                                      Selah

²⁰Our God *is* the God of salvation;
And to GOD the Lord *belong* escapes from death.

Celebrate the Lord's coming victory over His enemies. In Israel's court anticipate the glorious court of God in the heavens, and praise Him.

²¹But God will wound the head of His enemies,
The hairy scalp of the one who still goes on in his
    trespasses.
²²The Lord said, "I will bring back from Bashan,
I will bring *them* back from the depths of the sea,
²³That your foot may crush *them* in blood,
And the tongues of your dogs *may have* their portion
    from *your* enemies."

²⁴They have seen Your procession, O God,
The procession of my God, my King, into the
    sanctuary.
²⁵The singers went before, the players on instruments
    followed after;
Among *them were* the maidens playing timbrels.
²⁶Bless God in the congregations,
The Lord, from the fountain of Israel.
²⁷There *is* little Benjamin, their leader,
The princes of Judah *and* their company,
The princes of Zebulun *and* the princes of Naphtali.

²⁸Your God has commanded your strength;
Strengthen, O God, what You have done for us.
²⁹Because of Your temple at Jerusalem,
Kings will bring presents to You.
³⁰Rebuke the beasts of the reeds,
The herd of bulls with the calves of the peoples,
Till everyone submits himself with pieces of silver.
Scatter the peoples *who* delight in war.
³¹Envoys will come out of Egypt;
Ethiopia will quickly stretch out her hands to God.

154

Praise the sovereign God of our salvation!

³²Sing to God, you kingdoms of the earth;
Oh, sing praises to the Lord,

Selah

³³To Him who rides on the heaven of heavens, *which were* of old!
Indeed, He sends out His voice, a mighty voice.
³⁴Ascribe strength to God;
His excellence *is* over Israel,
And His strength *is* in the clouds.
³⁵O God, *You are* more awesome than Your holy places.
The God of Israel *is* He who gives strength and power to *His* people.

Blessed *be* God!

Psalm 69

Through various trials David expresses his confidence in the Lord and trusts Him to deal with his enemies. Praise Jesus for suffering for our sin, and look to Him for faith to bear up under trial. Read Matthew 27:32–50.

To the Chief Musician. Set to "The Lilies." *A Psalm* of David.

Thank the Lord, who paid our debt in His own body on the cross. Seek His strength in times of trouble.

¹Save me, O God!
For the waters have come up to *my* neck.
²I sink in deep mire,
Where *there* is no standing;

155

I have come into deep waters,
Where the floods overflow me.
³I am weary with my crying;
My throat is dry;
My eyes fail while I wait for my God.

⁴Those who hate me without a cause
Are more than the hairs of my head;
They are mighty who would destroy me,
Being my enemies wrongfully;
Though I have stolen nothing,
I *still* must restore *it*.

Thank Jesus for bearing your sins. Repent out of gratitude to Him.

⁵O God, You know my foolishness;
And my sins are not hidden from You.
⁶Let not those who wait for You,
    O Lord GOD of hosts, be ashamed because of me;
Let not those who seek You be confounded because
    of me,
    O God of Israel.
⁷Because for Your sake I have borne reproach;
Shame has covered my face.
⁸I have become a stranger to my brothers,
And an alien to my mother's children;
⁹Because zeal for Your house has eaten me up,
And the reproaches of those who reproach You have
    fallen on me.
¹⁰When I wept *and chastened* my soul with fasting,
That became my reproach.
¹¹I also made sackcloth my garment;
I became a byword to them.
¹²Those who sit in the gate speak against me,
And I *am* the song of the drunkards.

Like Jesus on the cross, seek God's help in bearing up under adversity.

[13]But as for me, my prayer *is* to You,
O Lord, *in* the acceptable time;
O God, in the multitude of Your mercy,
Hear me in the truth of Your salvation.
[14]Deliver me out of the mire,
And let me not sink;
Let me be delivered from those who hate me,
And out of the deep waters.
[15]Let not the floodwater overflow me,
Nor let the deep swallow me up;
And let not the pit shut its mouth on me.

[16]Hear me, O Lord, for Your lovingkindness is good;
Turn to me according to the multitude of Your tender
mercies.
[17]And do not hide Your face from Your servant,
For I am in trouble;
Hear me speedily.
[18]Draw near to my soul, *and* redeem it;
Deliver me because of my enemies.

Review your sufferings before the Lord, and grieve for the sufferings we cause Him.

[19]You know my reproach, my shame, and my
dishonor;
My adversaries *are* all before You.
[20]Reproach has broken my heart,
And I am full of heaviness;
I looked *for someone* to take pity, but *there was* none;
And for comforters, but I found none.
[21]They also gave me gall for my food,
And for my thirst they gave me vinegar to drink.

Trust the Lord to deal with those who torment you, whether men or spirits.

²²Let their table become a snare before them,
And their well-being a trap.
²³Let their eyes be darkened, so that they do not see;
And make their loins shake continually.
²⁴Pour out Your indignation upon them,
And let Your wrathful anger take hold of them.
²⁵Let their habitation be desolate;
Let no one dwell in their tents.
²⁶For they persecute *him* whom You have struck,
And talk of the grief of those You have wounded.
²⁷Add iniquity to their iniquity,
And let them not come into Your righteousness.
²⁸Let them be blotted out of the book of the living,
And not be written with the righteous.

Praise and thank the Lord, as Jesus did, even in the midst of your suffering.

²⁹But I *am* poor and sorrowful;
Let Your salvation, O God, set me up on high.
³⁰I will praise the name of God with a song,
And will magnify Him with thanksgiving.
³¹*This* also shall please the LORD better than an ox *or* bull,
Which has horns and hooves.
³²The humble shall see *this and* be glad;
And you who seek God, your hearts shall live.
³³For the LORD hears the poor,
And does not despise His prisoners.

³⁴Let heaven and earth praise Him,
The seas and everything that moves in them.
³⁵For God will save Zion
And build the cities of Judah,
That they may dwell there and possess it.

³⁶Also, the descendants of His servants shall inherit it,
And those who love His name shall dwell in it.

Psalm 70

*In this brief psalm of complaint, David cries out for help
against unnamed foes. Use it to pray for yourself or others
who are struggling with opposition or oppression of any kind.
Read Revelation 2:8–11.*

To the Chief Musician. *A Psalm* of David. To bring to remembrance.

Seek God's intervention against your enemies, or those of His people.

¹*Make haste*, O God, to deliver me!
Make haste to help me, O Lᴏʀᴅ!

²Let them be ashamed and confounded
Who seek my life;
Let them be turned back and confused
Who desire my hurt.
³Let them be turned back because of their shame,
Who say, "Aha, aha!"

Seek the joy of the Lord in the midst of your trial, and magnify Him.

⁴Let all those who seek You rejoice and be glad in
   You;
And let those who love Your salvation say continually,
"Let God be magnified!"

Present your specific needs—or those of others—to the Lord, and seek His help.

> ⁵But I *am* poor and needy;
> Make haste to me, O God!
> You *are* my help and my deliverer;
> O Lord, do not delay.

Psalm 71

This psalm of testimony and praise appears to be from one who has entered into the later years of his life. Believers of any age can use it to seek God's protection, recall His goodness, invoke His blessings, and praise Him for His grace. Read Ephesians 3:14–21.

Declare your confidence in the Lord.

> ¹In You, O Lord, I put my trust;
> Let me never be put to shame.
> ²Deliver me in Your righteousness, and cause me to escape;
> Incline Your ear to me, and save me.
> ³Be my strong habitation,
> To which I may resort continually;
> You have given the commandment to save me,
> For You *are* my rock and my fortress.

Present your specific need before the Lord, and seek His help. Recall the ways He has faithfully helped you in the past.

> ⁴Deliver me, O my God, out of the hand of the wicked,
> Out of the hand of the unrighteous and cruel man.

5For You are my hope, O Lord GOD;
You are my trust from my youth.
6By You I have been upheld from *my* birth;
You are He who took me out of my mother's womb.
My praise *shall be* continually of You.

7I have become as a wonder to many,
But You *are* my strong refuge.
8Let my mouth be filled *with* Your praise
And with Your glory all the day.

Call upon the Lord to intervene against those who trouble you, whether men or spirits.

9Do not cast me off in the time of old age;
Do not forsake me when my strength fails.
10For my enemies speak against me;
And those who lie in wait for my life take counsel
     together,
11Saying, "God has forsaken him;
Pursue and take him, for *there is* none to deliver *him*."

12O God, do not be far from me;
O my God, make haste to help me!
13Let them be confounded *and* consumed
Who are adversaries of my life;
Let them be covered *with* reproach and dishonor
Who seek my hurt.

Resolve to hope in the Lord and to declare His salvation.

14But I will hope continually,
And will praise You yet more and more.
15My mouth shall tell of Your righteousness
And Your salvation all the day,
For I do not know *their* limits.

[16]I will go in the strength of the Lord God;
I will make mention of Your righteousness, of Yours
only.

Thank the Lord for past blessings, and seek His reviving grace.

[17]O God, You have taught me from my youth;
And to this *day* I declare Your wondrous works.
[18]Now also when I *am* old and gray-headed,
O God, do not forsake me,
Until I declare Your strength to *this* generation,
Your power to everyone *who* is to come.

[19]Also Your righteousness, O God, *is* very high,
You who have done great things;
O God, who *is* like You?
[20]*You,* who have shown me great and severe troubles,
Shall revive me again,
And bring me up again from the depths of the earth.
[21]You shall increase my greatness,
And comfort me on every side.

Praise the Lord, and resolve to talk of Him with others.

[22]Also with the lute I will praise You—
And Your faithfulness, O my God!
To You I will sing with the harp,
O Holy One of Israel.
[23]My lips shall greatly rejoice when I sing to You,
And my soul, which You have redeemed.
[24]My tongue also shall talk of Your righteousness all
the day long;
For they are confounded,
For they are brought to shame
Who seek my hurt.

Psalm 72

*This psalm may well recall Solomon's prayer for wisdom in
2 Chronicles 1:6–12. While this psalm leads us to praise the
righteous rule of King Jesus, it can also be useful in praying
for civil magistrates, as well as church leaders. Read 1 Timothy 2:1–4.*

A Psalm of Solomon.

Ask God to give wisdom to civil governors, that righteousness and justice may prevail in the land under the eye of King Jesus.

¹Give the king Your judgments, O God,
And Your righteousness to the king's Son.
²He will judge Your people with righteousness,
And Your poor with justice.
³The mountains will bring peace to the people,
And the little hills, by righteousness.
⁴He will bring justice to the poor of the people;
He will save the children of the needy,
And will break in pieces the oppressor.

⁵They shall fear You
As long as the sun and moon endure,
Throughout all generations.
⁶He shall come down like rain upon the mown grass,
Like showers *that* water the earth.
⁷In His days the righteous shall flourish,
And abundance of peace,
Until the moon is no more.

Pray for the increase of God's kingdom and of the rule and authority of righteous magistrates.

⁸He shall have dominion also from sea to sea,
And from the River to the ends of the earth.

⁹Those who dwell in the wilderness will bow before
   Him,
And His enemies will lick the dust.
¹⁰The kings of Tarshish and of the isles
Will bring presents;
The kings of Sheba and Seba
Will offer gifts.
¹¹Yes, all kings shall fall down before Him;
All nations shall serve Him.

Praise God for His tender care of the needy, and ask Him to give civil magistrates similar compassion.

¹²For He will deliver the needy when he cries,
The poor also, and *him* who has no helper.
¹³He will spare the poor and needy,
And will save the souls of the needy.
¹⁴He will redeem their life from oppression and
   violence;
And precious shall be their blood in His sight.

Pray that God's people may prosper under the rule of King Jesus, and that the land may be prosperous and at peace under wise rulers.

¹⁵And He shall live;
And the gold of Sheba will be given to Him;
Prayer also will be made for Him continually,
And daily He shall be praised.

¹⁶There will be an abundance of grain in the earth,
On the top of the mountains;
Its fruit shall wave like Lebanon;
And *those* of the city shall flourish like grass of the
   earth.

Praise the name of Jesus, and bless Him for His wondrous rule.

> [17]His name shall endure forever;
> His name shall continue as long as the sun.
> And *men* shall be blessed in Him;
> All nations shall call Him blessed.
>
> [18]Blessed *be* the LORD God, the God of Israel,
> Who only does wondrous things!
> [19]And blessed *be* His glorious name forever!
> And let the whole earth be filled *with* His glory.
> Amen and Amen.
>
> [20]The prayers of David the son of Jesse are ended.

Psalm 73

Asaph describes his battle with temptation in this psalm of testimony. We can use it to examine our hearts and to prepare for the temptations we face each day. Read 1 Corinthians 10:6–13.

A Psalm of Asaph.

Present to the Lord those areas in which you are often tempted.

> [1]Truly God *is* good to Israel,
> To such as are pure in heart.
> [2]But as for me, my feet had almost stumbled;
> My steps had nearly slipped.
> [3]For I *was* envious of the boastful,
> When I saw the prosperity of the wicked.

⁴For *there are* no pangs in their death,
But their strength *is* firm.
⁵They *are* not in trouble *as other* men,
Nor are they plagued like *other* men.
⁶Therefore pride serves as their necklace;
Violence covers them *like* a garment.
⁷Their eyes bulge with abundance;
They have more than heart could wish.
⁸They scoff and speak wickedly *concerning*
    oppression;
They speak loftily.
⁹They set their mouth against the heavens,
And their tongue walks through the earth.

¹⁰Therefore his people return here,
And waters of a full *cup* are drained by them.
¹¹And they say, "How does God know?
And is there knowledge in the Most High?"
¹²Behold, these *are* the ungodly,
Who are always at ease;
They increase *in* riches.
¹³Surely I have cleansed my heart *in* vain,
And washed my hands in innocence.
¹⁴For all day long I have been plagued,
And chastened every morning.

Resist temptation by recalling your duty to the community of faith.

¹⁵If I had said, "I will speak thus,"
Behold, I would have been untrue to the generation
    of Your children.

Allow your being tempted to trouble you and to bring you into the presence of God.

¹⁶When I thought *how* to understand this,
It *was* too painful for me—

[17]Until I went into the sanctuary of God;
Then I understood their end.

Recall the slippery nature of sin and the end of sinners.

[18]Surely You set them in slippery places;
You cast them down to destruction.
[19]Oh, how they are *brought* to desolation, as in a
moment!
They are utterly consumed with terrors.
[20]As a dream when *one* awakes,
So, Lord, when You awake,
You shall despise their image.

Grieve to be thus tempted, to be so like a mere beast; but rejoice to be ever in the presence of God.

[21]Thus my heart was grieved,
And I was vexed in my mind.
[22]I *was* so foolish and ignorant;
I was *like* a beast before You.
[23]Nevertheless I *am* continually with You;
You hold *me* by my right hand.
[24]You will guide me with Your counsel,
And afterward receive me *to* glory.

Rest in the goodness and sufficiency of God in the face of temptation.

[25]Whom have I in heaven *but You?*
And *there is* none upon earth *that* I desire besides
You.
[26]My flesh and my heart fail;
But God *is* the strength of my heart and my portion
forever.

²⁷For indeed, those who are far from You shall perish;
You have destroyed all those who desert You for
harlotry.
²⁸But *it is* good for me to draw near to God;
I have put my trust in the Lord GOD,
That I may declare all Your works.

Psalm 74

In this psalm of complaint Asaph seems to foresee the violence of the nations against the people of Israel and the temple of the Lord. We may use this psalm to pray about ways we or the church may have compromised with the world and are thus being destroyed by it. Read Romans 12:1–2.

A Contemplation of Asaph.

Reflect on any ways in which you or your church may be compromising with worldliness. Consider the damage this is causing.

¹O God, why have You cast *us* off forever?
Why does Your anger smoke against the sheep of
Your pasture?
²Remember Your congregation, *which* You have
purchased of old,
The tribe of Your inheritance, *which* You have
redeemed—
This Mount Zion where You have dwelt.
³Lift up Your feet to the perpetual desolations.
The enemy has damaged everything in the sanctuary.
⁴Your enemies roar in the midst of Your meeting
place;

⁵They set up banners *for* signs.
They seem like men who lift up
Axes among the thick trees.
⁶And now they break down its carved work, all at
    once,
With axes and hammers.
⁷They have set fire to Your sanctuary;
They have defiled the dwelling place of Your name to
    the ground.
⁸They said in their hearts,
"Let us destroy them altogether."
They have burned up all the meeting places of God
    in the land.

**Cry out to God to deliver His church from
oppression and worldliness, recalling His might
and power.**

⁹We do not see our signs;
There is no longer any prophet;
Nor *is there* any among us who knows how long.
¹⁰O God, how long will the adversary reproach?
Will the enemy blaspheme Your name forever?
¹¹Why do You withdraw Your hand, even Your right
    hand?
Take it out of Your bosom and destroy *them.*
¹²For God *is* my King from of old,
Working salvation in the midst of the earth.
¹³You divided the sea by Your strength;
You broke the heads of the sea serpents in the waters.
¹⁴You broke the heads of Leviathan in pieces,
And gave him as food to the people inhabiting the
    wilderness.
¹⁵You broke open the fountain and the flood;
You dried up mighty rivers.
¹⁶The day *is* Yours, the night also *is* Yours;
You have prepared the light and the sun.

[17]You have set all the borders of the earth;
You have made summer and winter.

[18]Remember this, *that* the enemy has reproached, O
    LORD,
And *that* a foolish people has blasphemed Your name.
[19]Oh, do not deliver the life of Your turtledove to the
    wild beast!
Do not forget the life of Your poor forever.
[20]Have respect to the covenant;
For the dark places of the earth are full of the
    habitations of cruelty.
[21]Oh, do not let the oppressed return ashamed!
Let the poor and needy praise Your name.

[22]Arise, O God, plead Your own cause;
Remember how the foolish man reproaches You daily.
[23]Do not forget the voice of Your enemies;
The tumult of those who rise up against You
    increases continually.

Psalm 75

In this psalm of testimony and praise, Asaph confidently declares his trust in the Lord and His justice against the wicked. Use this psalm to nurture patience until the coming of the Lord in salvation and judgment. Read Revelation 22:6–17.

To the Chief Musician. Set to "Do Not Destroy." A Psalm of Asaph. A Song.

Give thanks to God as you recall His many wondrous works.

[1]We give thanks to You, O God, we give thanks!
For Your wondrous works declare *that* Your name is
    near.

Thank the Lord for His coming judgment and salvation.

²"When I choose the proper time, I will judge
   uprightly.
³The earth and all its inhabitants are dissolved;
I set up its pillars firmly.

Selah

⁴"I said to the boastful, 'Do not deal boastfully,'
And to the wicked, 'Do not lift up the horn.
⁵Do not lift up your horn on high;
Do *not* speak with a stiff neck.' "

⁶For exaltation *comes* neither from the east
Nor from the west nor from the south.
⁷But God *is* the Judge:
He puts down one,
And exalts another.
⁸For in the hand of the Lᴏʀᴅ *there is* a cup,
And the wine is red;
It is full mixed, and He pours it out;
Surely its dregs shall all the wicked of the earth
Drain *and* drink down.

Resolve to declare the praises of God and His coming judgment.

⁹But I will declare forever,
I will sing praises to the God of Jacob.

¹⁰"All the horns of the wicked I will also cut off,
But the horns of the righteous shall be exalted."

Psalm 76

In this psalm of praise and celebration, Asaph rejoices in the Lord's peace and His victory over all His foes. Pray this psalm to renew your commitment to the Lord and to look forward to His final victory over His enemies and ours. Read 1 Corinthians 15:20–28.

To the Chief Musician. On stringed instruments. A Psalm of Asaph. A Song.

Thank the Lord for His presence with us and for His peace.

¹In Judah God *is* known;
His name *is* great in Israel.
²In Salem also is His tabernacle,
And His dwelling place in Zion.
³There He broke the arrows of the bow,
The shield and the sword of battle.

Selah

Praise God for Christ's victory over His foes.

⁴You *are* more glorious and excellent
Than the mountains of prey.
⁵The stouthearted were plundered;
They have sunk into their sleep;
And none of the mighty men have found the use of
their hands.
⁶At Your rebuke, O God of Jacob,
Both the chariot and horses were cast into a dead
sleep.

Exalt the Lord in His power and greatness.

⁷You, Yourself, *are* to be feared;
And who may stand in Your presence
When once You are angry?

⁸You caused judgment to be heard from heaven;
The earth feared and was still,
⁹When God arose to judgment,
To deliver all the oppressed of the earth.

Selah

Recommit yourself to the Lord, and offer to Him sacrifices of thanks and praise.

¹⁰Surely the wrath of man shall praise You;
With the remainder of wrath You shall gird Yourself.
¹¹Make vows to the LORD your God, and pay *them;*
Let all who are around Him bring presents to Him
who ought to be feared.
¹²He shall cut off the spirit of princes;
He is awesome to the kings of the earth.

Psalm 77

Asaph offers a psalm of complaint, seeking renewal in the Lord and celebrating His might and shepherding care. Use this psalm to ask the Lord to return His favor to His people, that they might be renewed in Him. Read Hebrews 11:32–12:1.

To the Chief Musician. To Jeduthun. A Psalm of Asaph.

Spread your anguish and your concerns before the Lord; seek Him earnestly.

¹I cried out to God with my voice—
To God with my voice;
And He gave ear to me.

²In the day of my trouble I sought the Lord;
My hand was stretched out in the night without
    ceasing;
My soul refused to be comforted.
³I remembered God, and was troubled;
I complained, and my spirit was overwhelmed.

                                             Selah

⁴You hold my eyelids *open;*
I am so troubled that I cannot speak.
⁵I have considered the days of old,
The years of ancient times.
⁶I call to remembrance my song in the night;
I meditate within my heart,
And my spirit makes diligent search.

Plead with God to show His mercy once again.

⁷Will the Lord cast off forever?
And will He be favorable no more?
⁸Has His mercy ceased forever?
Has *His* promise failed forevermore?
⁹Has God forgotten to be gracious?
Has He in anger shut up His tender mercies?

                                             Selah

Recall the many works of grace and power that God has shown in the past.

¹⁰And I said, "This *is* my anguish;
But I will remember the years of the right hand of the
    Most High."
¹¹I will remember the works of the LORD;
Surely I will remember Your wonders of old.
¹²I will also meditate on all Your work,
And talk of Your deeds.
¹³Your way, O God, *is* in the sanctuary;
Who *is* so great a God as *our* God?

¹⁴You *are* the God who does wonders;
You have declared Your strength among the peoples.
¹⁵You have with *Your* arm redeemed Your people,
The sons of Jacob and Joseph.

Selah

Rejoice in the mighty power of God, and call on Him to shepherd His people again.

¹⁶The waters saw You, O God;
The waters saw You, they were afraid;
The depths also trembled.
¹⁷The clouds poured out water;
The skies sent out a sound;
Your arrows also flashed about.
¹⁸The voice of Your thunder was in the whirlwind;
The lightnings lit up the world;
The earth trembled and shook.
¹⁹Your way *was* in the sea,
Your path in the great waters,
And Your footsteps were not known.
²⁰You led Your people like a flock
By the hand of Moses and Aaron.

Psalm 78

In this psalm of testimony Asaph recalls Israel's history and rests in the shepherding care of the Lord. Pray this psalm on behalf of the church, that it might hear the voice of the Lord and be delivered from the many failings of His people in the past. Read Hebrews 6.

A Contemplation of Asaph.

Pray that God will bless His teachers and preachers and give His people ears to hear.

¹Give ear, O my people, *to* my law;
Incline your ears to the words of my mouth.
²I will open my mouth in a parable;
I will utter dark sayings of old,
³Which we have heard and known,
And our fathers have told us.
⁴We will not hide *them* from their children,
Telling to the generation to come the praises of the
    LORD,
And His strength and His wonderful works that He
    has done.

⁵For He established a testimony in Jacob,
And appointed a law in Israel,
Which He commanded our fathers,
That they should make them known to their
    children;
⁶That the generation to come might know *them,*
The children *who* would be born,
That they may arise and declare *them* to their
    children,
⁷That they may set their hope in God,
And not forget the works of God,
But keep His commandments;

[8]And may not be like their fathers,
A stubborn and rebellious generation,
A generation *that* did not set its heart aright,
And whose spirit was not faithful to God.

Recall Israel's sin and pray that God would deliver His church from neglect of our mission.

[9]The children of Ephraim, *being* armed *and* carrying
   bows,
Turned back in the day of battle.
[10]They did not keep the covenant of God;
They refused to walk in His law,
[11]And forgot His works
And His wonders that He had shown them.

Recall the grace of God in delivering us through Christ, just as He delivered Israel.

[12]Marvelous things He did in the sight of their
   fathers,
In the land of Egypt, *in* the field of Zoan.
[13]He divided the sea and caused them to pass
   through;
And He made the waters stand up like a heap.
[14]In the daytime also He led them with the cloud,
And all the night with a light of fire.
[15]He split the rocks in the wilderness,
And gave *them* drink in abundance like the depths.
[16]He also brought streams out of the rock,
And caused waters to run down like rivers.

Recall Israel's sin and pray that God would deliver His church from selfish desires and requests.

[17]But they sinned even more against Him
By rebelling against the Most High in the wilderness.
[18]And they tested God in their heart
By asking for the food of their fancy.

¹⁹Yes, they spoke against God:
They said: "Can God prepare a table in the
    wilderness?
²⁰Behold, He struck the rock,
So that the waters gushed out,
And the streams overflowed.
Can He give bread also?
Can He provide meat for His people?"

²¹Therefore the Lord heard *this* and was furious;
So a fire was kindled against Jacob,
And anger also came up against Israel,
²²Because they did not believe in God,
And did not trust in His salvation.
²³Yet He had commanded the clouds above,
And opened the doors of heaven,
²⁴Had rained down manna on them to eat,
And given them of the bread of heaven.
²⁵Men ate angels' food;
He sent them food to the full.

²⁶He caused an east wind to blow in the heavens;
And by His power He brought in the south wind.
²⁷He also rained meat on them like the dust,
Feathered fowl like the sand of the seas;
²⁸And He let *them* fall in the midst of their camp,
All around their habitations.
²⁹So they ate and were well filled,
For He gave them their own desire.
³⁰They were not deprived of their craving;
But while their food *was* still in their mouths,
³¹The wrath of God came against them,
And slew the stoutest of them,
And struck down the choice *men* of Israel.

Recall Israel's sin and pray that God will protect His church from merely superficial faith.

³²In spite of this they still sinned,
And did not believe in His wondrous works.
³³Therefore their days He consumed in futility,
And their years in fear.

³⁴When He slew them, then they sought Him;
And they returned and sought diligently for God.
³⁵Then they remembered that God *was* their rock,
And the Most High God their redeemer.
³⁶Nevertheless they flattered Him with their mouth,
And they lied to Him with their tongue;
³⁷For their heart was not steadfast with Him,
Nor were they faithful in His covenant.
³⁸But He, *being* full of compassion, forgave *their*
  iniquity,
And did not destroy *them.*
Yes, many a time He turned His anger away,
And did not stir up all His wrath;
³⁹For He remembered that they *were but* flesh,
A breath that passes away and does not come again.

Pray that God's people would not forget His mighty works, but remember to praise Him ever.

⁴⁰How often they provoked Him in the wilderness,
And grieved Him in the desert!
⁴¹Yes, again and again they tempted God,
And limited the Holy One of Israel.
⁴²They did not remember His power:
The day when He redeemed them from the enemy,
⁴³When He worked His signs in Egypt,
And His wonders in the field of Zoan;
⁴⁴Turned their rivers into blood,
And their streams, that they could not drink.

[45]He sent swarms of flies among them, which
    devoured them,
And frogs, which destroyed them.
[46]He also gave their crops to the caterpillar,
And their labor to the locust.
[47]He destroyed their vines with hail,
And their sycamore trees with frost.
[48]He also gave up their cattle to the hail,
And their flocks to fiery lightning.
[49]He cast on them the fierceness of His anger,
Wrath, indignation, and trouble,
By sending angels of destruction *among them*.
[50]He made a path for His anger;
He did not spare their soul from death,
But gave their life over to the plague,
[51]And destroyed all the firstborn in Egypt,
The first of *their* strength in the tents of Ham.
[52]But He made His own people go forth like sheep,
And guided them in the wilderness like a flock;
[53]And He led them on safely, so that they did not fear;
But the sea overwhelmed their enemies.
[54]And He brought them to His holy border,
The mountain *which* His right hand had acquired.
[55]He also drove out the nations before them,
Allotted them an inheritance by survey,
And made the tribes of Israel dwell in their tents.

Recall Israel's sin and pray that God would preserve His church from idolatry.

[56]Yet they tested and provoked the Most High God,
And did not keep His testimonies,
[57]But turned back and acted unfaithfully like their
    fathers;
They turned aside like a deceitful bow.
[58]For they provoked Him to anger with their high
    places,

And moved Him to jealousy with their carved
    images.
⁵⁹When God heard *this,* He was furious,
And greatly abhorred Israel,
⁶⁰So that He forsook the tabernacle of Shiloh,
The tent *which* He had placed among men,
⁶¹And delivered His strength into captivity,
And His glory into the enemy's hand.
⁶²He also gave His people over to the sword,
And was furious with His inheritance.
⁶³The fire consumed their young men,
And their maidens were not given in marriage.
⁶⁴Their priests fell by the sword,
And their widows made no lamentation.

**Call out to the Lord to revive His people and to
give them faithful shepherds, like David.**

⁶⁵Then the Lord awoke as *one out of* sleep,
And like a mighty man who shouts because of wine.
⁶⁶And He beat back His enemies;
He put them to a perpetual reproach.

⁶⁷Moreover He rejected the tent of Joseph,
And did not choose the tribe of Ephraim,
⁶⁸But chose the tribe of Judah,
Mount Zion which He loved.
⁶⁹And He built His sanctuary like the heights,
Like the earth which He has established forever.
⁷⁰He also chose David His servant,
And took him from the sheepfolds;
⁷¹From following the ewes that had young He
    brought him,
To shepherd Jacob His people,
And Israel His inheritance.
⁷²So he shepherded them according to the integrity of
    his heart,
And guided them by the skillfulness of his hands.

Psalm 79

In this psalm of complaint Asaph seeks the Lord's deliverance from unknown enemies. Use this psalm to pray for the church, either in persecution or where it is succumbing to worldly influences. Read Revelation 3:18–29.

A Psalm of Asaph.

Remember the persecuted church. Ask the Lord to show you any ways that the world has "invaded" your church.

¹O God, the nations have come into Your inheritance;
Your holy temple they have defiled;
They have laid Jerusalem in heaps.
²The dead bodies of Your servants
They have given *as* food for the birds of the heavens,
The flesh of Your saints to the beasts of the earth.
³Their blood they have shed like water all around
        Jerusalem,
And *there was* no one to bury *them.*
⁴We have become a reproach to our neighbors,
A scorn and derision to those who are around us.

Call upon God to show mercy to His people.

⁵How long, LORD?
Will You be angry forever?
Will Your jealousy burn like fire?
⁶Pour out Your wrath on the nations that do not
        know You,
And on the kingdoms that do not call on Your name.
⁷For they have devoured Jacob,
And laid waste his dwelling place.

**Confess any sins—yours or those of the church—
that may be standing in the way of God's blessing.**

⁸Oh, do not remember former iniquities against us!
Let Your tender mercies come speedily to meet us,
For we have been brought very low.
⁹Help us, O God of our salvation,
For the glory of Your name;
And deliver us, and provide atonement for our sins,
For Your name's sake!
¹⁰Why should the nations say,
"Where *is* their God?"
Let there be known among the nations in our sight
The avenging of the blood of Your servants *which has
been* shed.

**Seek God's help for specific sufferers, and give
Him thanks and praise.**

¹¹Let the groaning of the prisoner come before You;
According to the greatness of Your power
Preserve those who are appointed to die;
¹²And return to our neighbors sevenfold into their
bosom
Their reproach with which they have reproached
You, O Lord.

¹³So we, Your people and sheep of Your pasture,
Will give You thanks forever;
We will show forth Your praise to all generations.

Psalm 80

In yet another psalm of complaint, Asaph calls on the Lord to revive and restore His people. We can use this psalm in just the same way, to seek God's renewing grace for His church. Read 1 Corinthians 1:4–9.

To the Chief Musician. Set to "The Lilies." A Testimony of Asaph. A Psalm.

Pray that God would stir up His Spirit to revive His church.

¹Give ear, O Shepherd of Israel,
You who lead Joseph like a flock;
You who dwell *between* the cherubim, shine forth!
²Before Ephraim, Benjamin, and Manasseh,
Stir up Your strength,
And come *and* save us!

³Restore us, O God;
Cause Your face to shine,
And we shall be saved!

Pray that God would bring His people to tears of repentance, and that He would hear their prayers.

⁴O LORD God of hosts,
How long will You be angry
Against the prayer of Your people?
⁵You have fed them with the bread of tears,
And given them tears to drink in great measure.
⁶You have made us a strife to our neighbors,
And our enemies laugh among themselves.

⁷Restore us, O God of hosts;
Cause Your face to shine,
And we shall be saved!

Recall God's grace to His church in the past; consider its current state.

[8]You have brought a vine out of Egypt;
You have cast out the nations, and planted it.
[9]You prepared *room* for it,
And caused it to take deep root,
And it filled the land.
[10]The hills were covered with its shadow,
And the mighty cedars with its boughs.
[11]She sent out her boughs to the Sea,
And her branches to the River.

[12]Why have You broken down her hedges,
So that all who pass by the way pluck her *fruit?*
[13]The boar out of the woods uproots it,
And the wild beast of the field devours it.

Call upon God to strengthen and revive His church.

[14]Return, we beseech You, O God of hosts;
Look down from heaven and see,
And visit this vine
[15]And the vineyard which Your right hand has
    planted,
And the branch *that* You made strong for Yourself.
[16]*It is* burned with fire, *it is* cut down;
They perish at the rebuke of Your countenance.
[17]Let Your hand be upon the man of Your right hand,
Upon the son of man *whom* You made strong for
    Yourself.
[18]Then we will not turn back from You;
Revive us, and we will call upon Your name.

[19]Restore us, O LORD God of hosts;
Cause Your face to shine,
And we shall be saved!

Psalm 81

This psalm combines elements of testimony and admonition to call Israel to heed the Word of the Lord. We can pray it in just the same way for ourselves and the church today. Read Revelation 3:12–17.

To the Chief Musician. On an instrument of Gath. *A Psalm* of Asaph.

Praise and worship God, as is right and as He has called us to do.

> [1]Sing aloud to God our strength;
> Make a joyful shout to the God of Jacob,
> [2]Raise a song and strike the timbrel,
> The pleasant harp with the lute.
>
> [3]Blow the trumpet at the time of the New Moon,
> At the full moon, on our solemn feast day.
> [4]For this *is* a statute for Israel,
> *And* a law of the God of Jacob.
> [5]This He established in Joseph *for* a testimony,
> When He went throughout the land of Egypt,
> *Where* I heard a language *that* I did not understand.

Recall God's grace in delivering us from guilt and sin.

> [6]"I removed his shoulder from the burden;
> His hands were freed from the baskets.
> [7]You called in trouble, and I delivered you;
> I answered you in the secret place of thunder;
> I proved you at the waters of Meribah.

Selah

Pray that God's people would hear and heed His Word.

[8]"Hear, O My people, and I will admonish you!
O Israel, if you will listen to Me!
[9]There shall be no foreign god among you;
Nor shall you worship any foreign god.
[10]I *am* the LORD your God,
Who brought you out of the land of Egypt;
Open your mouth wide, and I will fill it.

[11]"But My people would not heed My voice,
And Israel would *have* none of Me.
[12]So I gave them over to their own stubborn heart,
To walk in their own counsels.

Pray that God's people would seek Him only.

[13]"Oh, that My people would listen to Me,
That Israel would walk in My ways!
[14]I would soon subdue their enemies,
And turn My hand against their adversaries.
[15]The haters of the LORD would pretend submission
    to Him,
But their fate would endure forever.
[16]He would have fed them also with the finest of
    wheat;
And with honey from the rock I would have satisfied
    you."

Psalm 82

Asaph complains of the injustice of Israel's leaders. Use this psalm to ask God to give the leaders of His people wisdom, understanding, and righteous judgment. Read 1 Timothy 3:1–13.

A Psalm of Asaph.

Pray that God's leaders would judge with righteous judgment.

¹God stands in the congregation of the mighty;
He judges among the gods.
²How long will you judge unjustly,
And show partiality to the wicked?

Selah

³Defend the poor and fatherless;
Do justice to the afflicted and needy.
⁴Deliver the poor and needy;
Free *them* from the hand of the wicked.

Ask God to remind His leaders of their high calling and to judge the world righteously through them.

⁵They do not know, nor do they understand;
They walk about in darkness;
All the foundations of the earth are unstable.

⁶I said, "You *are* gods,
And all of you *are* children of the Most High.
⁷But you shall die like men,
And fall like one of the princes."

⁸Arise, O God, judge the earth;
For You shall inherit all the nations.

Psalm 83

*In this psalm of imprecation Asaph calls down the judgment
of God against Israel's enemies. Pray that God would intervene on behalf of His church against all its persecutors. Read
Revelation 6:9–17.*

A Song. A Psalm of Asaph.

**Call upon the Lord to see the wickedness of those
who persecute His people.**

¹Do not keep silent, O God!
Do not hold Your peace,
And do not be still, O God!
²For behold, Your enemies make a tumult;
And those who hate You have lifted up their head.
³They have taken crafty counsel against Your people,
And consulted together against Your sheltered ones.
⁴They have said, "Come, and let us cut them off from
   being a nation,
That the name of Israel may be remembered no
   more."

**Bring to the Lord specific instances of persecution,
and seek His help.**

⁵For they have consulted together with one *consent;*
They form a confederacy against You:
⁶The tents of Edom and the Ishmaelites;
Moab and the Hagrites;
⁷Gebal, Ammon, and Amalek;
Philistia with the inhabitants of Tyre;
⁸Assyria also has joined with them;
They have helped the children of Lot.

Selah

Pray that God would turn His enemies to seek Him or would nullify their power, to the praise of His name.

⁹Deal with them as *with* Midian,
As *with* Sisera,
As *with* Jabin at the Brook Kishon,
¹⁰Who perished at Endor,
Who became *as* refuse on the earth.
¹¹Make their nobles like Oreb and like Zeeb,
Yes, all their princes like Zebah and Zalmunna,
¹²Who said, "Let us take for ourselves
The pastures of God for a possession."

¹³O my God, make them like the whirling dust,
Like the chaff before the wind!
¹⁴As the fire burns the woods,
And as the flame sets the mountains on fire,
¹⁵So pursue them with Your tempest,
And frighten them with Your storm.
¹⁶Fill their faces with shame,
That they may seek Your name, O LORD.
¹⁷Let them be confounded and dismayed forever;
Yes, let them be put to shame and perish,
¹⁸That *men* may know that You, whose name alone *is* the LORD,
Are the Most High over all the earth.

Psalm 84

In this psalm of praise the psalmists celebrate the dwelling of God with His people. Use it to rejoice in the Lord, who has promised never to leave us. Read Matthew 28:18–20; Hebrews 13:5.

To the Chief Musician. On an instrument of Gath. A Psalm of the sons of Korah.

Ask the Lord to create in you a desire to be ever in His presence.

¹How lovely *is* Your tabernacle,
O LORD of hosts!
²My soul longs, yes, even faints
For the courts of the LORD;
My heart and my flesh cry out for the living God.

Ask the Lord to let you dwell in His house.

³Even the sparrow has found a home,
And the swallow a nest for herself,
Where she may lay her young—
Even Your altars, O LORD of hosts,
My King and my God.
⁴Blessed *are* those who dwell in Your house;
They will still be praising You.

Selah

Seek the Lord's strength and grace to sustain you in trouble.

⁵Blessed *is* the man whose strength *is* in You,
Whose heart *is* set on pilgrimage.
⁶*As they* pass through the Valley of Baca,
They make it a spring;
The rain also covers it with pools.
⁷They go from strength to strength;
Every one of them appears before God in Zion.

Seek the presence of God, and resolve to rest in and glorify Him throughout the day.

⁸O LORD God of hosts, hear my prayer;
Give ear, O God of Jacob!

Selah

⁹O God, behold our shield,
And look upon the face of Your anointed.

¹⁰For a day in Your courts *is* better than a thousand.
I would rather be a doorkeeper in the house of my
    God
Than dwell in the tents of wickedness.
¹¹For the LORD God *is* a sun and shield;
The LORD will give grace and glory;
No good *thing* will He withhold
From those who walk uprightly.

¹²O LORD of hosts,
Blessed *is* the man who trusts in You!

Psalm 85

This psalm has elements of complaint and testimony, as the psalmists call on God to revive His people. Pray that God will revive His church today, as He has done so often in the past. Read 2 Corinthians 4:1–15.

To the Chief Musician. A Psalm of the sons of Korah.

Praise God for the way He has often revived His church, as He did Israel.

¹LORD, You have been favorable to Your land;
You have brought back the captivity of Jacob.
²You have forgiven the iniquity of Your people;
You have covered all their sin.

                          Selah

³You have taken away all Your wrath;
You have turned from the fierceness of Your anger.

Pray that God will revive His church.

⁴Restore us, O God of our salvation,
And cause Your anger toward us to cease.
⁵Will You be angry with us forever?
Will You prolong Your anger to all generations?
⁶Will You not revive us again,
That Your people may rejoice in You?
⁷Show us Your mercy, O LORD,
And grant us Your salvation.

Listen for how the Lord may be leading you in this work of revival. Pray that His people may hear Him.

⁸I will hear what God the LORD will speak,
For He will speak peace
To His people and to His saints;
But let them not turn back to folly.
⁹Surely His salvation *is* near to those who fear Him,
That glory may dwell in our land.

Praise the Lord that, in Jesus, mercy and truth, righteousness and peace have met together. Seek His reviving grace.

¹⁰Mercy and truth have met together;
Righteousness and peace have kissed *each other.*
¹¹Truth shall spring out of the earth,
And righteousness shall look down from heaven.
¹²Yes, the LORD will give *what is* good;
And our land will yield its increase.
¹³Righteousness will go before Him,
And shall make His footsteps *our* pathway.

Psalm 86

In this psalm of complaint David cries out for the Lord to show him mercy in the midst of distress. Use it to seek God's help in your time of need or that of others. Read Hebrews 4:14–16.

A Prayer of David.

Seek mercy and forgiveness for your sins.

¹Bow down Your ear, O LORD, hear me;
For I *am* poor and needy.
²Preserve my life, for I *am* holy;
You are my God;
Save Your servant who trusts in You!
³Be merciful to me, O Lord,
For I cry to You all day long.
⁴Rejoice the soul of Your servant,
For to You, O Lord, I lift up my soul.
⁵For You, Lord, *are* good, and ready to forgive,
And abundant in mercy to all those who call upon
You.

Ask God to hear your prayer, and praise His greatness.

⁶Give ear, O LORD, to my prayer;
And attend to the voice of my supplications.
⁷In the day of my trouble I will call upon You,
For You will answer me.

⁸Among the gods *there is* none like You, O Lord;
Nor *are there any works* like Your works.
⁹All nations whom You have made
Shall come and worship before You, O Lord,
And shall glorify Your name.

¹⁰For You *are* great, and do wondrous things;
You alone *are* God.

**Seek the Lord's guidance, and resolve to praise
Him more and more.**

¹¹Teach me Your way, O Lᴏʀᴅ;
I will walk in Your truth.
Unite my heart to fear Your name.
¹²I will praise You, O Lord my God, with all my heart,
And I will glorify Your name forevermore.
¹³For great *is* Your mercy toward me,
And You have delivered my soul from the depths of
    Sheol.

**Bring your specific requests, or those of others, to
the Lord, and seek His help.**

¹⁴O God, the proud have risen against me,
And a mob of violent *men* have sought my life,
And have not set You before them.
¹⁵But You, O Lord, *are* a God full of compassion, and
    gracious,
Longsuffering and abundant in mercy and truth.

¹⁶Oh, turn to me, and have mercy on me!
Give Your strength to Your servant,
And save the son of Your maidservant.
¹⁷Show me a sign for good,
That those who hate me may see *it* and be ashamed,
Because You, Lᴏʀᴅ, have helped me and comforted
    me.

Psalm 87

This psalm of testimony exalts the city of Jerusalem and the God of Israel over the surrounding nations and peoples. Use it to pray for church leaders and for the gathering of the nations to Jesus. Read Acts 1:8.

A Psalm of the sons of Korah. A Song.

Praise the unchangeable, holy God. Intercede for church leaders—those who "sit in the gates"—to know His love and to spread it among His people.

¹His foundation *is* in the holy mountains.
²The LORD loves the gates of Zion
More than all the dwellings of Jacob.
³Glorious things are spoken of you,
O city of God!

Selah

Pray for the nations to be brought into the church with joy and rejoicing.

⁴"I will make mention of Rahab and Babylon to those
    who know Me;
Behold, O Philistia and Tyre, with Ethiopia:
'This *one* was born there.'"

⁵And of Zion it will be said,
"This *one* and that *one* were born in her;
And the Most High Himself shall establish her."
⁶The LORD will record,
When He registers the peoples:
"This one was born there."

Selah

⁷Both the singers and the players on instruments *say,*
"All my springs *are* in you."

Psalm 88

This psalm of complaint speaks to the despondency and despair of the human soul. Use it to seek relief in your times of trouble, or to intercede for others in their dark night of the soul. Read 1 Corinthians 12:26.

A Song. A Psalm of the sons of Korah. To the Chief Musician. Set to "Mahalath Leannoth." A Contemplation of Heman the Ezrahite.

Pray that those who suffer may persevere in seeking the Lord.

¹O LORD, God of my salvation,
I have cried out day and night before You.
²Let my prayer come before You;
Incline Your ear to my cry.

Ask God to be near to those who suffer.

³For my soul is full of troubles,
And my life draws near to the grave.
⁴I am counted with those who go down to the pit;
I am like a man *who ha*s no strength,
⁵Adrift among the dead,
Like the slain who lie in the grave,
Whom You remember no more,
And who are cut off from Your hand.

Pray that God may relieve their suffering.

⁶You have laid me in the lowest pit,
In darkness, in the depths.
⁷Your wrath lies heavy upon me,
And You have afflicted *me* with all Your waves.

Selah

[8]You have put away my acquaintances far from me;
You have made me an abomination to them;
I *am* shut up, and I cannot get out;
[9]My eye wastes away because of affliction.

Pray that those who suffer may yet remember God's purpose for them.

LORD, I have called daily upon You;
I have stretched out my hands to You.
[10]Will You work wonders for the dead?
Shall the dead arise *and* praise You?

Selah

[11]Shall Your lovingkindness be declared in the grave?
Or Your faithfulness in the place of destruction?
[12]Shall Your wonders be known in the dark?
And Your righteousness in the land of forgetfulness?

Pray that God will be with and strengthen all those who suffer.

[13]But to You I have cried out, O LORD,
And in the morning my prayer comes before You.
[14]LORD, why do You cast off my soul?
Why do You hide Your face from me?
[15]I *have been* afflicted and ready to die from *my* youth
    up;
I suffer Your terrors;
I am distraught.
[16]Your fierce wrath has gone over me;
Your terrors have cut me off.
[17]They came around me all day long like water;
They engulfed me altogether.
[18]Loved one and friend You have put far from me,
And my acquaintances into darkness.

Psalm 89

*This is a psalm of testimony and complaint, reviewing God's
faithfulness and Israel's need for revival. We can use it in just
the same way, recalling God's goodness to His covenant people
and seeking His renewing grace. Read Hebrews 11:32–40.*

A Contemplation of Ethan the Ezrahite.

Praise God for His mercy and faithfulness.

¹I will sing of the mercies of the LORD forever;
With my mouth will I make known Your faithfulness
    to all generations.
²For I have said,
    "Mercy shall be built up forever;
Your faithfulness You shall establish in the very
    heavens."

³"I have made a covenant with My chosen,
I have sworn to My servant David:
⁴"Your seed I will establish forever,
And build up your throne to all generations.' "

                                      Selah

Praise God for His greatness and might.

⁵And the heavens will praise Your wonders, O LORD;
Your faithfulness also in the congregation of the
    saints.
⁶For who in the heavens can be compared to the
    LORD?
Who among the sons of the mighty can be likened to
    the LORD?
⁷God is greatly to be feared in the assembly of the
    saints,
And to be held in reverence by all *those who ar*e
    around Him.

[8]O Lord God of hosts,
Who *is* mighty like You, O Lord?
Your faithfulness also surrounds You.
[9]You rule the raging of the sea;
When its waves rise, You still them.
[10]You have broken Rahab in pieces, as one who is
slain;
You have scattered Your enemies with Your mighty
arm.

Praise God for His blessings to His people.

[11]The heavens *are* Yours, the earth also is Yours;
The world and all its fullness, You have founded
them.
[12]The north and the south, You have created them;
Tabor and Hermon rejoice in Your name.
[13]You have a mighty arm;
Strong is Your hand, *and* high is Your right hand.
[14]Righteousness and justice *are* the foundation of
Your throne;
Mercy and truth go before Your face.
[15]Blessed *are* the people who know the joyful sound!
They walk, O Lord, in the light of Your countenance.
[16]In Your name they rejoice all day long,
And in Your righteousness they are exalted.
[17]For You *are* the glory of their strength,
And in Your favor our horn is exalted.
[18]For our shield *belongs* to the Lord,
And our king to the Holy One of Israel.

Praise God for His covenant with David, fulfilled in Christ.

[19]Then You spoke in a vision to Your holy one,
And said: "I have given help to *one who is* mighty;
I have exalted one chosen from the people.

²⁰I have found My servant David;
With My holy oil I have anointed him,
²¹With whom My hand shall be established;
Also My arm shall strengthen him.
²²The enemy shall not outwit him,
Nor the son of wickedness afflict him.
²³I will beat down his foes before his face,
And plague those who hate him.

²⁴"But My faithfulness and My mercy *shall be* with
    him,
And in My name his horn shall be exalted.
²⁵Also I will set his hand over the sea,
And his right hand over the rivers.
²⁶He shall cry to Me, 'You *are* my Father,
My God, and the rock of my salvation.'
²⁷Also I will make him *My* firstborn,
The highest of the kings of the earth.
²⁸My mercy I will keep for him forever,
And My covenant shall stand firm with him.
²⁹His seed also I will make *to endure* forever,
And his throne as the days of heaven.

Pray that God's people may be faithful in keeping His covenant.

³⁰"If his sons forsake My law
And do not walk in My judgments,
³¹If they break My statutes
And do not keep My commandments,
³²Then I will visit their transgression with the rod,
And their iniquity with stripes.
³³Nevertheless My lovingkindness I will not utterly
    take from him,
Nor allow My faithfulness to fail.
³⁴My covenant I will not break,
Nor alter the word that has gone out of My lips.

³⁵Once I have sworn by My holiness;
I will not lie to David:
³⁶His seed shall endure forever,
And his throne as the sun before Me;
³⁷It shall be established forever like the moon,
Even *like* the faithful witness in the sky."

Selah

Intercede for God's people in their unfaithfulness and distress.

³⁸But You have cast off and abhorred,
You have been furious with Your anointed.
³⁹You have renounced the covenant of Your servant;
You have profaned his crown *by casting it* to the
    ground.
⁴⁰You have broken down all his hedges;
You have brought his strongholds to ruin.
⁴¹All who pass by the way plunder him;
He is a reproach to his neighbors.
⁴²You have exalted the right hand of his adversaries;
You have made all his enemies rejoice.
⁴³You have also turned back the edge of his sword,
And have not sustained him in the battle.
⁴⁴You have made his glory cease,
And cast his throne down to the ground.
⁴⁵The days of his youth You have shortened;
You have covered him with shame.

Selah

Pray that God would intervene to revive His languishing church.

⁴⁶How long, LORD?
Will You hide Yourself forever?
Will Your wrath burn like fire?

⁴⁷Remember how short my time is;
For what futility have You created all the children of
    men?
⁴⁸What man can live and not see death?
Can he deliver his life from the power of the grave?

                                                    Selah

⁴⁹Lord, where *are* Your former lovingkindnesses,
Which You swore to David in Your truth?
⁵⁰Remember, Lord, the reproach of Your servants—
How I bear in my bosom *the reproach of* all the many
    peoples,
⁵¹With which Your enemies have reproached, O
    Lᴏʀᴅ,
With which they have reproached the footsteps of
    Your anointed.

⁵²Blessed *be* the Lᴏʀᴅ forevermore!
Amen and Amen.

Psalm 90

*Moses seeks God's help in the work appointed to him. Use this
psalm to seek God's help in the stewardship of your time and
responsibilities. Read Ephesians 5:15–17; Colossians 3:23–24.*

A Prayer of Moses the man of God.

Praise the Lord, our eternal, unchangeable dwelling place.

¹Lord, You have been our dwelling place in all
    generations.
²Before the mountains were brought forth,
Or ever You had formed the earth and the world,
Even from everlasting to everlasting, You *are* God.

Thank the Lord for your brief time on earth.

³You turn man to destruction,
And say, "Return, O children of men."
⁴For a thousand years in Your sight
Are like yesterday when it is past,
And like a watch in the night.
⁵You carry them away *like* a flood;
They are like a sleep.
In the morning they are like grass *which* grows up;
⁶In the morning it flourishes and grows up;
In the evening it is cut down and withers.

Pray that your days may not be spent in sin, but wisely.

⁷For we have been consumed by Your anger,
And by Your wrath we are terrified.
⁸You have set our iniquities before You,
Our secret *sins* in the light of Your countenance.
⁹For all our days have passed away in Your wrath;
We finish our years like a sigh.
¹⁰The days of our lives *are* seventy years;
And if by reason of strength *they are* eighty years,
Yet their boast *is* only labor and sorrow;
For it is soon cut off, and we fly away.
¹¹Who knows the power of Your anger?
For as the fear of You, *so is* Your wrath.
¹²So teach *us* to number our days,
That we may gain a heart of wisdom.

Seek God's mercy and gladness in all your work this day.

¹³Return, O LORD!
How long?
And have compassion on Your servants.

¹⁴Oh, satisfy us early with Your mercy,
That we may rejoice and be glad all our days!
¹⁵Make us glad according to the days *in which* You
  have afflicted us,
And the years *in which* we have seen evil.
¹⁶Let Your work appear to Your servants,
And Your glory to their children.
¹⁷And let the beauty of the LORD our God be upon us,
And establish the work of our hands for us;
Yes, establish the work of our hands.

Psalm 91

This psalm testifies to the protection God affords all who take shelter in Him. We should easily be able to adapt it to our own needs. Read John 16:33.

Commit to taking refuge in the Lord in the face of temptation and adversity.

¹He who dwells in the secret place of the Most High
Shall abide under the shadow of the Almighty.
²I will say of the LORD, "*He is* my refuge and my
  fortress;
My God, in Him I will trust."

Praise God for His protection, and look to Him to deliver you from fear.

³Surely He shall deliver you from the snare of the
  fowler
And from the perilous pestilence.
⁴He shall cover you with His feathers,
And under His wings you shall take refuge;
His truth *shall be your* shield and buckler.

⁵You shall not be afraid of the terror by night,
Nor of the arrow *that* flies by day,
⁶*Nor* of the pestilence *that* walks in darkness,
Nor of the destruction *that* lays waste at noonday.

⁷A thousand may fall at your side,
And ten thousand at your right hand;
But it shall not come near you.
⁸Only with your eyes shall you look,
And see the reward of the wicked.

Thank God for protecting angels.

⁹Because you have made the LORD, *who is* my refuge,
Even the Most High, your habitation,
¹⁰No evil shall befall you,
Nor shall any plague come near your dwelling;
¹¹For He shall give His angels charge over you,
To keep you in all your ways.
¹²They shall bear you up in *their* hands,
Lest you dash your foot against a stone.
¹³You shall tread upon the lion and the cobra,
The young lion and the serpent you shall trample
    under foot.

Express your love for the Lord, and call upon Him to deliver you.

¹⁴"Because he has set his love upon Me, therefore I
    will deliver him;
I will set him on high, because he has known My
    name.
¹⁵He shall call upon Me, and I will answer him;
I *will be* with him in trouble;
I will deliver him and honor him.
¹⁶With long life I will satisfy him,
And show him My salvation."

Psalm 92

This psalm of testimony praises the greatness of God and His works and claims the promise of abundant life, even into old age. We may use it in just the same way. Read 2 Timothy 1:8–12.

A Psalm. A Song for the Sabbath day.

**Give thanks to God, and declare the many ways
He shows Himself faithful to us.**

> ¹*It is* good to give thanks to the LORD,
> And to sing praises to Your name, O Most High;
> ²To declare Your lovingkindness in the morning,
> And Your faithfulness every night,
> ³On an instrument of ten strings,
> On the lute,
> And on the harp,
> With harmonious sound.
> ⁴For You, LORD, have made me glad through Your
>   work;
> I will triumph in the works of Your hands.

Rehearse the many wonderful works of the Lord.

> ⁵O LORD, how great are Your works!
> Your thoughts are very deep.
> ⁶A senseless man does not know,
> Nor does a fool understand this.
> ⁷When the wicked spring up like grass,
> And when all the workers of iniquity flourish,
> *It is* that they may be destroyed forever.

**Extol the greatness of God and His victory over all
His foes.**

> ⁸But You, LORD, are on high forevermore.
> ⁹For behold, Your enemies, O LORD,

For behold, Your enemies shall perish;
All the workers of iniquity shall be scattered.

Thank the Lord for the ways He has exalted and blessed you.

[10]But my horn You have exalted like a wild ox;
I have been anointed with fresh oil.
[11]My eye also has seen *my desire* on my enemies;
My ears hear *my desire* on the wicked
Who rise up against me.

Pray that God would make you fruitful for Him.

[12]The righteous shall flourish like a palm tree,
He shall grow like a cedar in Lebanon.
[13]Those who are planted in the house of the LORD
Shall flourish in the courts of our God.
[14]They shall still bear fruit in old age;
They shall be fresh and flourishing,
[15]To declare that the LORD is upright;
He is my rock, and *there is* no unrighteousness in
Him.

Psalm 93

This psalm of praise celebrates the reign of God over all things. Use it to praise Christ, our King, and to trust Him in the face of trials. Read Philippians 2:5–11.

Praise God who rules over all.

[1]The LORD reigns, He is clothed with majesty;
The LORD is clothed,
He has girded Himself with strength.

Surely the world is established, so that it cannot be
  moved.
²Your throne *is* established from of old;
You *are* from everlasting.

Trust God to deliver you through the trials of each day.

³The floods have lifted up, O LORD,
The floods have lifted up their voice;
The floods lift up their waves.
⁴The LORD on high *is* mightier
Than the noise of many waters,
Than the mighty waves of the sea.

⁵Your testimonies are very sure;
Holiness adorns Your house,
O LORD, forever.

Psalm 94

This psalm of admonition and imprecation calls upon the Lord to judge the unrighteousness of men. Use it to seek God's help in spiritual warfare and to call upon Him to deliver His people from the hands of the wicked. Read Ephesians 6:10–20.

Call upon the Lord to stand forth against all His foes.

¹O LORD God, to whom vengeance belongs—
O God, to whom vengeance belongs, shine forth!
²Rise up, O Judge of the earth;
Render punishment to the proud.

³Lord, how long will the wicked,
How long will the wicked triumph?

Call upon God to behold the wickedness of men and evil spirits.

⁴They utter speech, *and* speak insolent things;
All the workers of iniquity boast in themselves.
⁵They break in pieces Your people, O Lord,
And afflict Your heritage.
⁶They slay the widow and the stranger,
And murder the fatherless.
⁷Yet they say, "The Lord does not see,
Nor does the God of Jacob understand."

Call upon God to cause the wicked to understand His sovereignty and omniscience.

⁸Understand, you senseless among the people;
And *you* fools, when will you be wise?
⁹He who planted the ear, shall He not hear?
He who formed the eye, shall He not see?
¹⁰He who instructs the nations, shall He not correct,
He who teaches man knowledge?
¹¹The Lord knows the thoughts of man,
That they *are* futile.

Seek God's help for those who suffer at the hands of the wicked.

¹²Blessed *is* the man whom You instruct, O Lord,
And teach out of Your law,
¹³That You may give him rest from the days of
    adversity,
Until the pit is dug for the wicked.
¹⁴For the Lord will not cast off His people,
Nor will He forsake His inheritance.

[15]But judgment will return to righteousness,
And all the upright in heart will follow it.

Seek the Lord's help for your own struggles with wickedness each day.

[16]Who will rise up for me against the evildoers?
Who will stand up for me against the workers of
    iniquity?
[17]Unless the LORD *had been* my help,
My soul would soon have settled in silence.
[18]If I say, "My foot slips,"
Your mercy, O LORD, will hold me up.
[19]In the multitude of my anxieties within me,
Your comforts delight my soul.

Declare your confidence in God.

[20]Shall the throne of iniquity, which devises evil by
    law,
Have fellowship with You?
[21]They gather together against the life of the
    righteous,
And condemn innocent blood.
[22]But the LORD has been my defense,
And my God the rock of my refuge.
[23]He has brought on them their own iniquity,
And shall cut them off in their own wickedness;
The LORD our God shall cut them off.

Psalm 95

We can use this psalm of praise to celebrate the greatness of God and to prepare our hearts to receive His Word. Read Hebrews 4:1–12.

Praise God for His greatness.

> ¹Oh come, let us sing to the LORD!
> Let us shout joyfully to the Rock of our salvation.
> ²Let us come before His presence with thanksgiving;
> Let us shout joyfully to Him with psalms.
> ³For the LORD *is* the great God,
> And the great King above all gods.
> ⁴In His hand *are* the deep places of the earth;
> The heights of the hills *are* His also.
> ⁵The sea *is* His, for He made it;
> And His hands formed the dry *land.*

Worship God, who has made you one of His own people.

> ⁶Oh come, let us worship and bow down;
> Let us kneel before the LORD our Maker.
> ⁷For He *is* our God,
> And we *are* the people of His pasture,
> And the sheep of His hand.

Pray that God will make your heart receptive to His Word.

> Today, if you will hear His voice:
> ⁸"Do not harden your hearts, as in the rebellion,
> *And* as *in* the day of trial in the wilderness,
> ⁹When your fathers tested Me;
> They proved Me, though they saw My work.
> ¹⁰For forty years I was grieved with *that* generation,
> And said, 'It *is* a people who go astray in their hearts,
> And they do not know My ways.'

¹¹So I swore in My wrath,
'They shall not enter My rest.' "

Psalm 96

This psalm of praise can be very helpful in leading us to worship God, to renew our mandate to the nations, and to anticipate His return in judgment. Read Acts 1:7–11.

Pray that praise to God and the proclamation of His salvation would increase on the earth.

¹Oh, sing to the LORD a new song!
Sing to the LORD, all the earth.
²Sing to the LORD, bless His name;
Proclaim the good news of His salvation from day to
   day.
³Declare His glory among the nations,
His wonders among all peoples.

Praise God for His greatness and majesty.

⁴For the LORD *is* great and greatly to be praised;
He *is* to be feared above all gods.
⁵For *all* the gods of the peoples *are* idols,
But the LORD made the heavens.
⁶Honor and majesty *are* before Him;
Strength and beauty *are* in His sanctuary.

⁷Give to the LORD, O kindreds of the peoples,
⁸Give to the LORD glory and strength.
Give to the LORD the glory *due* His name;
Bring an offering, and come into His courts.
⁹Oh, worship the LORD in the beauty of holiness!
Tremble before Him, all the earth.

Ask God to renew His people for the work of evangelism and missions.

[10]Say among the nations, "The LORD reigns;
The world also is firmly established,
It shall not be moved;
He shall judge the peoples righteously."

Rejoice in the promised coming of the Lord in judgment.

[11]Let the heavens rejoice, and let the earth be glad;
[12]Let the sea roar, and all its fullness;
Let the field be joyful, and all that is in it.
Then all the trees of the woods will rejoice [13]before
the LORD.
For He is coming, for He is coming to judge the
earth.
He shall judge the world with righteousness,
And the peoples with His truth.

Psalm 97

This is a psalm of testimony and admonition, warning God's people, in the light of His holiness, to turn away from evil. We can pray this in just the same way for ourselves and our churches. Read Ephesians 5:1–14.

Declare the sovereignty and greatness of God.

[1]The LORD reigns;
Let the earth rejoice;
Let the multitude of the isles be glad!

²Clouds and darkness surround Him;
Righteousness and justice *are* the foundation of His
    throne.
³A fire goes before Him,
And burns up His enemies round about.
⁴His lightnings light the world;
The earth sees and trembles.
⁵The mountains melt like wax at the presence of the
    Lord,
At the presence of the Lord of the whole earth.
⁶The heavens declare His righteousness,
And all the peoples see His glory.

Pray that God's people will turn away from all idolatry and all wickedness.

⁷Let all be put to shame who serve carved images,
Who boast of idols.
Worship Him, all *you* gods.
⁸Zion hears and is glad,
And the daughters of Judah rejoice
Because of Your judgments, O Lord.
⁹For You, Lord, *are* most high above all the earth;
You are exalted far above all gods.

¹⁰You who love the Lord, hate evil!

Praise the Lord, who keeps us from evil, and seek the light of His path.

He preserves the souls of His saints;
He delivers them out of the hand of the wicked.
¹¹Light is sown for the righteous,
And gladness for the upright in heart.
¹²Rejoice in the Lord, you righteous,
And give thanks at the remembrance of His holy
    name.

Psalm 98

This psalm praises the greatness of God and looks forward to the day of His coming again in judgment. Read Revelation 22:12–17.

A Psalm.

Praise God for His mighty works, especially His salvation.

¹Oh, sing to the LORD a new song!
For He has done marvelous things;
His right hand and His holy arm have gained Him
  the victory.
²The LORD has made known His salvation;
His righteousness He has openly shown in the sight
  of the nations.
³He has remembered His mercy and His faithfulness
  to the house of Israel;
All the ends of the earth have seen the salvation of
  our God.

Pray that praise to God would increase on the earth.

⁴Shout joyfully to the LORD, all the earth;
Break forth in song, rejoice, and sing praises.
⁵Sing to the LORD with the harp,
With the harp and the sound of a psalm,
⁶With trumpets and the sound of a horn;
Shout joyfully before the LORD, the King.

Pray with rejoicing in anticipation of the Lord's return in judgment.

⁷Let the sea roar, and all its fullness,
The world and those who dwell in it;

⁸Let the rivers clap *their* hands;
Let the hills be joyful together ⁹before the LORD,
For He is coming to judge the earth.
With righteousness He shall judge the world,
And the peoples with equity.

Psalm 99

This psalm praises God's greatness and recalls great leaders who served God's people. Use it to praise the Lord and to pray for church leaders. Read Colossians 4:2–6.

Praise God for His greatness and majesty.

¹The LORD reigns;
Let the peoples tremble!
He dwells *between* the cherubim;
Let the earth be moved!
²The LORD *is* great in Zion,
And He *is* high above all the peoples.
³Let them praise Your great and awesome name—
He *is* holy.

Pray that righteousness, justice, and the worship of God might increase.

⁴The King's strength also loves justice;
You have established equity;
You have executed justice and righteousness in Jacob.
⁵Exalt the LORD our God,
And worship at His footstool;
For He *is* holy.

Recall with gratitude great leaders of God's people, and pray for those who lead us today.

⁶Moses and Aaron were among His priests,
And Samuel was among those who called upon His
    name;
They called upon the Lord, and He answered them.
⁷He spoke to them in the cloudy pillar;
They kept His testimonies and the ordinance *that* He
    gave them.

⁸You answered them, O Lord our God;
You were to them God-Who-Forgives,
Though You took vengeance on their deeds.
⁹Exalt the Lord our God,
And worship at His holy hill;
For the Lord our God is holy.

Psalm 100

Use this psalm of thanksgiving to recall the many ways God has blessed you, and to praise and thank Him. Read Ephesians 1:3–14.

A Psalm of Thanksgiving.

Praise the greatness of God, our Creator, Redeemer, and Shepherd.

¹Make a joyful shout to the Lord, all you lands!
²Serve the Lord with gladness;
Come before His presence with singing.
³Know that the Lord, He *is* God;
It is He *who* has made us, and not we ourselves;
We are His people and the sheep of His pasture.

Give thanks to God for all His goodness, mercy, and truth.

> [4]Enter into His gates with thanksgiving,
> *And* into His courts with praise.
> Be thankful to Him, *and* bless His name.
> [5]For the LORD *is* good;
> His mercy *is* everlasting,
> And His truth *endures* to all generations.

Psalm 101

This psalm of David is a wisdom psalm. We can use it to review our walk with the Lord or to prepare for the day ahead. Read Ephesians 5:15–17.

A Psalm of David.

Greet the Lord with praise for His mercy and justice.

> [1]I will sing of mercy and justice;
> To You, O LORD, I will sing praises.

Review various aspects of your life before the Lord, and commit your way to Him.

> [2]I will behave wisely in a perfect way.
> Oh, when will You come to me?
> I will walk within my house with a perfect heart.
>
> [3]I will set nothing wicked before my eyes;
> I hate the work of those who fall away;
> It shall not cling to me.
> [4]A perverse heart shall depart from me;
> I will not know wickedness.

⁵Whoever secretly slanders his neighbor,
Him I will destroy;
The one who has a haughty look and a proud heart,
Him I will not endure.

⁶My eyes *shall be* on the faithful of the land,
That they may dwell with me;
He who walks in a perfect way,
He shall serve me.
⁷He who works deceit shall not dwell within my
house;
He who tells lies shall not continue in my presence.

Confess and repent of any known sin.

⁸Early I will destroy all the wicked of the land,
That I may cut off all the evildoers from the city of
the Lord.

Psalm 102

*This is a psalm of complaint, appealing to God for help in
the midst of adversity. Use it to pray for yourself or others
who may be enduring some trial from the good hand of the
Lord. Read 1 Thessalonians 1:2–7.*

A Prayer of the afflicted, when he is overwhelmed and pours out his complaint before
the Lord.

Ask the Lord to hear your prayer and the prayers of all who suffer.

¹Hear my prayer, O Lord,
And let my cry come to You.

²Do not hide Your face from me in the day of my
trouble;
Incline Your ear to me;
In the day that I call, answer me speedily.

**Meditate on the experience of suffering, either
your own or that of others. Intercede for those
who suffer.**

³For my days are consumed like smoke,
And my bones are burned like a hearth.
⁴My heart is stricken and withered like grass,
So that I forget to eat my bread.
⁵Because of the sound of my groaning
My bones cling to my skin.
⁶I am like a pelican of the wilderness;
I am like an owl of the desert.
⁷I lie awake,
And am like a sparrow alone on the housetop.

⁸My enemies reproach me all day long,
And those who deride me swear an oath against me.
⁹For I have eaten ashes like bread,
And mingled my drink with weeping,
¹⁰Because of Your indignation and Your wrath;
For You have lifted me up and cast me away.
¹¹My days *are* like a shadow that lengthens,
And I wither away like grass.

**Declare your trust in the Lord to deliver you and
all who suffer for His sake, and to build His
church.**

¹²But You, O Lᴏʀᴅ, shall endure forever,
And the remembrance of Your name to all
generations.
¹³You will arise *and* have mercy on Zion;
For the time to favor her,

Yes, the set time, has come.
¹⁴For Your servants take pleasure in her stones,
And show favor to her dust.
¹⁵So the nations shall fear the name of the LORD,
And all the kings of the earth Your glory.
¹⁶For the LORD shall build up Zion;
He shall appear in His glory.
¹⁷He shall regard the prayer of the destitute,
And shall not despise their prayer.

¹⁸This will be written for the generation to come,
That a people yet to be created may praise the LORD.
¹⁹For He looked down from the height of His
     sanctuary;
From heaven the LORD viewed the earth,
²⁰To hear the groaning of the prisoner,
To loose those appointed to death,
²¹To declare the name of the LORD in Zion,
And His praise in Jerusalem,
²²When the peoples are gathered together,
And the kingdoms, to serve the LORD.

Pray that God will strengthen all who suffer, to the praise of His glorious works.

²³He weakened my strength in the way;
He shortened my days.
²⁴I said, "O my God,
Do not take me away in the midst of my days;
Your years *are* throughout all generations.
²⁵Of old You laid the foundations of the earth,
And the heavens *are* the work of Your hands.
²⁶They will perish, but You will endure;
Yes, all of them will grow old like a garment;
Like a cloak You will change them,
And they will be changed.
²⁷But You *are* the same,
And Your years will have no end.

²⁸The children of Your servants will continue,
And their descendants will be established before
 You."

Psalm 103

David praises God for all His many benefits and leads us to do the same. Read Romans 11:33–36.

A *Psalm* of David.

Praise God for His mercy, forgiveness, and daily provision.

¹Bless the LORD, O my soul;
And all that is within me, *bless* His holy name!
²Bless the LORD, O my soul,
And forget not all His benefits:
³Who forgives all your iniquities,
Who heals all your diseases,
⁴Who redeems your life from destruction,
Who crowns you with lovingkindness and tender
 mercies,
⁵Who satisfies your mouth with good *things,*
So that your youth is renewed like the eagle's.

Recall God's mercy to Israel, and reflect on His mercy to you.

⁶The LORD executes righteousness
And justice for all who are oppressed.
⁷He made known His ways to Moses,
His acts to the children of Israel.
⁸The LORD is merciful and gracious,
Slow to anger, and abounding in mercy.

⁹He will not always strive *with us,*
Nor will He keep *His anger* forever.
¹⁰He has not dealt with us according to our sins,
Nor punished us according to our iniquities.

¹¹For as the heavens are high above the earth,
So great is His mercy toward those who fear Him;
¹²As far as the east is from the west,
So far has He removed our transgressions from us.
¹³As a father pities *his* children,
So the LORD pities those who fear Him.
¹⁴For He knows our frame;
He remembers that we *are* dust.

¹⁵*As for* man, his days *are* like grass;
As a flower of the field, so he flourishes.
¹⁶For the wind passes over it, and it is gone,
And its place remembers it no more.
¹⁷But the mercy of the LORD *is* from everlasting to
     everlasting
On those who fear Him,
And His righteousness to children's children,
¹⁸To such as keep His covenant,
And to those who remember His commandments to
     do them.

**Praise God for His sovereign rule, and call upon
the angels to join in praising Him.**

¹⁹The LORD has established His throne in heaven,
And His kingdom rules over all.

²⁰Bless the LORD, you His angels,
Who excel in strength, who do His word,
Heeding the voice of His word.
²¹Bless the LORD, all *you* His hosts,
You ministers of His, who do His pleasure.

²²Bless the LORD, all His works,
In all places of His dominion.

Bless the LORD, O my soul!

Psalm 104

*This glorious psalm of praise for the works of God can be for
us a joyful reminder of His constant care and unfathomable
love. Read Ephesians 3:14–21.*

Praise the Lord for His majestic greatness.

¹Bless the LORD, O my soul!
O LORD my God, You are very great:
You are clothed with honor and majesty,
²Who cover *Yourself* with light as *with* a garment,
Who stretch out the heavens like a curtain.

³He lays the beams of His upper chambers in the
 waters,
Who makes the clouds His chariot,
Who walks on the wings of the wind,
⁴Who makes His angels spirits,
His ministers a flame of fire.

Praise God for His mighty work of creation.

⁵*You who* laid the foundations of the earth,
So *that* it should not be moved forever,
⁶You covered it with the deep as *with* a garment;
The waters stood above the mountains.
⁷At Your rebuke they fled;
At the voice of Your thunder they hastened away.

⁸They went up over the mountains;
They went down into the valleys,
To the place which You founded for them.
⁹You have set a boundary that they may not pass
   over,
That they may not return to cover the earth.

Praise God for His abundant provision for His creatures.

¹⁰He sends the springs into the valleys,
Which flow among the hills.
¹¹They give drink to every beast of the field;
The wild donkeys quench their thirst.
¹²By them the birds of the heavens have their
   habitation;
They sing among the branches.
¹³He waters the hills from His upper chambers;
The earth is satisfied with the fruit of Your works.

¹⁴He causes the grass to grow for the cattle,
And vegetation for the service of man,
That he may bring forth food from the earth,
¹⁵And wine *that* makes glad the heart of man,
Oil to make *his* face shine,
And bread *which* strengthens man's heart.
¹⁶The trees of the LORD are full *of sap,*
The cedars of Lebanon which He planted,
¹⁷Where the birds make their nests;
The stork has her home in the fir trees.
¹⁸The high hills *are* for the wild goats;
The cliffs are a refuge for the rock badgers.

¹⁹He appointed the moon for seasons;
The sun knows its going down.
²⁰You make darkness, and it is night,
In which all the beasts of the forest creep about.

²¹The young lions roar after their prey,
And seek their food from God.
²²*When* the sun arises, they gather together
And lie down in their dens.
²³Man goes out to his work
And to his labor until the evening.

Praise God for the glory of His many works and for His Spirit who attends them.

²⁴O Lᴏʀᴅ, how manifold are Your works!
In wisdom You have made them all.
The earth is full of Your possessions—
²⁵This great and wide sea,
In which *are* innumerable teeming things,
Living things both small and great.
²⁶There the ships sail about;
And there is that Leviathan
Which You have made to play there.

²⁷These all wait for You,
That You may give *them* their food in due season.
²⁸*What* You give them they gather in;
You open Your hand, they are filled with good.
²⁹You hide Your face, they are troubled;
You take away their breath, they die and return to
    their dust.
³⁰You send forth Your Spirit, they are created;
And You renew the face of the earth.

Praise the everlasting glory and sovereign goodness of God.

³¹May the glory of the Lᴏʀᴅ endure forever;
May the Lᴏʀᴅ rejoice in His works.
³²He looks on the earth, and it trembles;
He touches the hills, and they smoke.

³³I will sing to the LORD as long as I live;
I will sing praise to my God while I have my being.
³⁴May my meditation be sweet to Him;
I will be glad in the LORD.
³⁵May sinners be consumed from the earth,
And the wicked be no more.

Bless the LORD, O my soul!
Praise the LORD!

Psalm 105

This psalm celebrates the covenant faithfulness of God. We can pray this psalm in gratitude to God for our redemption and for the completion of His covenant in Jesus Christ. Read 2 Corinthians 1:19–21.

Praise God for His grace, greatness, and mighty works.

¹Oh, give thanks to the LORD!
Call upon His name;
Make known His deeds among the peoples.
²Sing to Him, sing psalms to Him;
Talk of all His wondrous works.
³Glory in His holy name;
Let the hearts of those rejoice who seek the LORD.
⁴Seek the LORD and His strength;
Seek His face evermore.
⁵Remember His marvelous works which He has
    done,
His wonders, and the judgments of His mouth,
⁶O seed of Abraham His servant,
You children of Jacob, His chosen ones!

Praise God for His lovingkindness in choosing Israel and in choosing us.

⁷He *is* the Lord our God;
His judgments *are* in all the earth.
⁸He has remembered His covenant forever,
The word *which* He commanded, for a thousand
     generations,
⁹*The covenant* which He made with Abraham,
And His oath to Isaac,
¹⁰And confirmed it to Jacob for a statute,
To Israel *for* an everlasting covenant,
¹¹Saying, "To You I will give the land of Canaan
As the allotment of your inheritance,"
¹²When they were *but* few in number,
Indeed very few, and strangers in it.

Praise God for His faithfulness in caring for Israel, as He does for us.

¹³When they went from one nation to another,
From *one* kingdom to another people,
¹⁴He permitted no one to do them wrong;
Yes, He reproved kings for their sakes,
¹⁵*Saying,* "Do not touch My anointed ones,
And do My prophets no harm."

¹⁶Moreover He called for a famine in the land;
He destroyed all the provision of bread.
¹⁷He sent a man before them—
Joseph—*who* was sold as a slave.
¹⁸They hurt his feet with fetters,
He was laid in irons.
¹⁹Until the time that his word came to pass,
The word of the Lord tested him.
²⁰The king sent and released him,
The ruler of the people let him go free.

²¹He made him lord of his house,
And ruler of all his possessions,
²²To bind his princes at his pleasure,
And teach his elders wisdom.

²³Israel also came into Egypt,
And Jacob sojourned in the land of Ham.
²⁴And He increased His people greatly,
And made them stronger than their enemies.
²⁵He turned their heart to hate His people,
To deal craftily with His servants.

Praise the Lord for His redemption of Israel and for our own redemption in Jesus Christ.

²⁶He sent Moses His servant,
And Aaron whom He had chosen.
²⁷They performed His signs among them,
And wonders in the land of Ham.
²⁸He sent darkness, and made *it* dark;
And they did not rebel against His word.
²⁹He turned their waters into blood,
And killed their fish.
³⁰Their land abounded with frogs,
Even in the chambers of their kings.
³¹He spoke, and there came swarms of flies,
And lice in all their territory.
³²He gave them hail for rain,
And flaming fire in their land.
³³He struck their vines also, and their fig trees,
And splintered the trees of their territory.
³⁴He spoke, and locusts came,
Young locusts without number,
³⁵And ate up all the vegetation in their land,
And devoured the fruit of their ground.
³⁶He also destroyed all the firstborn in their land,
The first of all their strength.

[37]He also brought them out with silver and gold,
And *there was* none feeble among His tribes.
[38]Egypt was glad when they departed,
For the fear of them had fallen upon them.

Praise God for His guidance and provision for His people, then and now.

[39]He spread a cloud for a covering,
And fire to give light in the night.
[40]*The people* asked, and He brought quail,
And satisfied them with the bread of heaven.
[41]He opened the rock, and water gushed out;
It ran in the dry places *like* a river.

Praise our faithful God, and rejoice in the inheritance He has laid up for us in Christ.

[42]For He remembered His holy promise,
And Abraham His servant.
[43]He brought out His people with joy,
His chosen ones with gladness.
[44]He gave them the lands of the Gentiles,
And they inherited the labor of the nations,
[45]That they might observe His statutes
And keep His laws.

Praise the LORD!

Psalm 106

This psalm celebrates the goodness of God in forgiving the sins of Israel and calls upon Him to renew His people. As you pray this, plead with the Lord to deliver His people from sin and to bring revival to His church. Read James 5:7–20.

Praise God for His goodness and mercy and for all His mighty works.

¹Praise the LORD!

Oh, give thanks to the LORD, for *He is* good!
For His mercy *endures* forever.
²Who can utter the mighty acts of the LORD?
Or can declare all His praise?
³Blessed *are* those who keep justice,
And he who does righteousness at all times!

Seek the favor of the Lord and to know more of His salvation.

⁴Remember me, O LORD, with the favor *You have toward* Your people;
Oh, visit me with your salvation,
⁵That I may see the benefit of Your chosen ones,
That I may rejoice in the gladness of Your nation,
That I may glory with Your inheritance.

Confess your sins and those of the church.

⁶We have sinned with our fathers,
We have committed iniquity,
We have done wickedly.
⁷Our fathers in Egypt did not understand Your wonders;
They did not remember the multitude of Your mercies,
But rebelled by the sea—the Red Sea.

Praise God for His faithfulness in saving His people.

[8]Nevertheless He saved them for His name's sake,
That He might make His mighty power known.
[9]He rebuked the Red Sea also, and it dried up;
So He led them through the depths,
As through the wilderness.
[10]He saved them from the hand of him who hated
them,
And redeemed them from the hand of the enemy.
[11]The waters covered their enemies;
There was not one of them left.
[12]Then they believed His words;
They sang His praise.

Pray that God would deliver His church from lust and envy.

[13]They soon forgot His works;
They did not wait for His counsel,
[14]But lusted exceedingly in the wilderness,
And tested God in the desert.
[15]And He gave them their request,
But sent leanness into their soul.

[16]When they envied Moses in the camp,
And Aaron the saint of the Lᴏʀᴅ,
[17]The earth opened up and swallowed Dathan,
And covered the faction of Abiram.
[18]A fire was kindled in their company;
The flame burned up the wicked.

Pray that God would keep us from idolatry of every kind.

[19]They made a calf in Horeb,
And worshiped the molded image.

²⁰Thus they changed their glory
Into the image of an ox that eats grass.
²¹They forgot God their Savior,
Who had done great things in Egypt,
²²Wondrous works in the land of Ham,
Awesome things by the Red Sea.
²³Therefore He said that He would destroy them,
Had not Moses His chosen one stood before Him in
    the breach,
To turn away His wrath, lest He destroy *them*.

Pray that God would deliver us from disobedience to our mission.

²⁴Then they despised the pleasant land;
They did not believe His word,
²⁵But murmured in their tents,
And did not heed the voice of the LORD.
²⁶Therefore He lifted up His hand *in an oath* against
    them,
To overthrow them in the wilderness,
²⁷To overthrow their descendants among the nations,
And to scatter them in the lands.

Pray that God would deliver His people from moral compromise.

²⁸They joined themselves also to Baal of Peor,
And ate sacrifices made to the dead.
²⁹Thus they provoked *Him* to anger with their deeds,
And the plague broke out among them.
³⁰Then Phinehas stood up and intervened,
And *so* the plague was stopped.
³¹And that was accounted to him for righteousness
To all generations forevermore.

Pray that God would quell grumbling among His people.

³²They angered *Him* also at the waters of strife,
So that it went ill with Moses on account of them;
³³Because they rebelled against His Spirit,
So that he spoke rashly with his lips.

Pray that God would deliver His church from worldly entanglements.

³⁴They did not destroy the peoples,
Concerning whom the Lord had commanded them,
³⁵But they mingled with the Gentiles
And learned their works;
³⁶They served their idols,
Which became a snare to them.
³⁷They even sacrificed their sons
And their daughters to the demons,
³⁸And shed innocent blood,
Even the blood of their sons and daughters,
Whom they sacrificed to the idols of Canaan;
And the land was polluted with blood.
³⁹Thus they were defiled by their own works,
And played the harlot by their own deeds.

Pray that God would stay His wrath from His people and deliver them from the oppression of their foes.

⁴⁰Therefore the wrath of the Lord was kindled against
    His people,
So that He abhorred His own inheritance.
⁴¹And He gave them into the hand of the Gentiles,
And those who hated them ruled over them.
⁴²Their enemies also oppressed them,
And they were brought into subjection under their
    hand.

⁴³Many times He delivered them;
But they rebelled *against Him* by their counsel,
And were brought low for their iniquity.

Praise and thank God for His faithfulness, and call upon Him to renew His church.

⁴⁴Nevertheless He regarded their affliction,
When He heard their cry;
⁴⁵And for their sake He remembered His covenant,
And relented according to the multitude of His
    mercies.
⁴⁶He also made them to be pitied
By all those who carried them away captive.

⁴⁷Save us, O Lord our God,
And gather us from among the Gentiles,
To give thanks to Your holy name,
And to triumph in Your praise.

⁴⁸Blessed *be* the Lord God of Israel
From everlasting to everlasting!
And let all the people say, "Amen!"

Praise the Lord!

Psalm 107

This psalm of thanksgiving and praise will lead you to declare the goodness of God for the many ways He has blessed you by His grace. Read 2 Corinthians 5:17–21.

Praise God for the redemption we have in Jesus.

¹Oh, give thanks to the LORD, for *He is* good!
For His mercy *endures* forever.
²Let the redeemed of the LORD say *so,*
Whom He has redeemed from the hand of the enemy,
³And gathered out of the lands,
From the east and from the west,
From the north and from the south.

Praise God for satisfying your hungry and thirsty soul. Intercede for lost friends.

⁴They wandered in the wilderness in a desolate way;
They found no city to dwell in.
⁵Hungry and thirsty,
Their soul fainted in them.
⁶Then they cried out to the LORD in their trouble,
And He delivered them out of their distresses.
⁷And He led them forth by the right way,
That they might go to a city for habitation.
⁸Oh, that *men* would give thanks to the LORD *for* His goodness,
And *for* His wonderful works to the children of men!
⁹For He satisfies the longing soul,
And fills the hungry soul with goodness.

Praise God, who has renewed your heart to love and serve Him. Pray for your lost friends and neighbors.

¹⁰Those who sat in darkness and in the shadow of death,
Bound in affliction and irons—
¹¹Because they rebelled against the words of God,
And despised the counsel of the Most High,
¹²Therefore He brought down their heart with labor;
They fell down, and *there was* none to help.

¹³Then they cried out to the Lord in their trouble,
And He saved them out of their distresses.
¹⁴He brought them out of darkness and the shadow of
   death,
And broke their chains in pieces.
¹⁵Oh, that *men* would give thanks to the Lord *for* His
   goodness,
And *for* His wonderful works to the children of men!
¹⁶For He has broken the gates of bronze,
And cut the bars of iron in two.

**Praise the Lord, who can deliver you from the love
of sinning. Intercede for lost neighbors and
friends.**

¹⁷Fools, because of their transgression,
And because of their iniquities, were afflicted.
¹⁸Their soul abhorred all manner of food,
And they drew near to the gates of death.
¹⁹Then they cried out to the Lord in their trouble,
And He saved them out of their distresses.
²⁰He sent His word and healed them,
And delivered *them* from their destructions.
²¹Oh, that *men* would give thanks to the Lord *for* His
   goodness,
And *for* His wonderful works to the children of men!
²²Let them sacrifice the sacrifices of thanksgiving,
And declare His works with rejoicing.

**Praise God for His mighty works, and plead with
Him to make Himself known to lost people.**

²³Those who go down to the sea in ships,
Who do business on great waters,
²⁴They see the works of the Lord,
And His wonders in the deep.
²⁵For He commands and raises the stormy wind,
Which lifts up the waves of the sea.

²⁶They mount up to the heavens,
They go down again to the depths;
Their soul melts because of trouble.
²⁷They reel to and fro, and stagger like a drunken
     man,
And are at their wits' end.
²⁸Then they cry out to the LORD in their trouble,
And He brings them out of their distresses.
²⁹He calms the storm,
So that its waves are still.
³⁰Then they are glad because they are quiet;
So He guides them to their desired haven.
³¹Oh, that *men* would give thanks to the LORD *for* His
     goodness,
And *for* His wonderful works to the children of men!
³²Let them exalt Him also in the congregation of the
     people,
And praise Him in the assembly of the elders.

Praise God for His justice and His faithful and abundant provision for all our needs.

³³He turns rivers into a wilderness,
And the watersprings into dry ground;
³⁴A fruitful land into barrenness,
For the wickedness of those who dwell in it.
³⁵He turns a wilderness into pools of water,
And dry land into watersprings.
³⁶There He makes the hungry dwell,
That they may establish a city for habitation,
³⁷And sow fields and plant vineyards,
That they may yield a fruitful harvest.
³⁸He also blesses them, and they multiply greatly;
And He does not let their cattle decrease.

³⁹When they are diminished and brought low
Through oppression, affliction, and sorrow,

⁴⁰He pours contempt on princes,
And causes them to wander in the wilderness *where
there is* no way;
⁴¹Yet He sets the poor on high, far from affliction,
And makes *their* families like a flock.
⁴²The righteous see *it* and rejoice,
And all iniquity stops its mouth.

⁴³Whoever *is* wise will observe these *things,*
And they will understand the lovingkindness of the
LORD.

Psalm 108

*Drawing on two earlier psalms (57, 60), David's psalm of
praise to God can lead us to rejoice in His steadfast love and
to call on Him to renew His people in their mission. Read
1 Corinthians 9:16–23.*

A Song. A Psalm of David.

Praise God for His mercy.

¹O God, my heart is steadfast;
I will sing and give praise, even with my glory.
²Awake, lute and harp!
I will awaken the dawn.
³I will praise You, O LORD, among the peoples,
And I will sing praises to You among the nations.
⁴For Your mercy *is* great above the heavens,
And Your truth *reaches* to the clouds.

⁵Be exalted, O God, above the heavens,
And Your glory above all the earth;
⁶That Your beloved may be delivered,
Save *with* Your right hand, and hear me.

Recall that God has given the nations to Jesus, who called us to preach the Good News of forgiveness to them.

⁷God has spoken in His holiness:
"I will rejoice;
I will divide Shechem
And measure out the Valley of Succoth.
⁸Gilead *is* Mine;
Manasseh *is* Mine;
Ephraim also *is* the helmet for My head;
Judah *is* My lawgiver.
⁹Moab *is* My washpot;
Over Edom I will cast My shoe;
Over Philistia I will triumph."

Plead with God to renew His church in the work of proclaiming His kingdom.

¹⁰Who will bring me into the strong city?
Who will lead me to Edom?
¹¹*Is it* not You, O God, *who* cast us off?
And You, O God, *who* did not go out with our
    armies?
¹²Give us help from trouble,
For vain *is* the help of man.
¹³Through God we shall do valiantly,
For *it is* He *who* shall tread down our enemies.

Psalm 109

In this psalm of complaint it is easy to see the betrayal and suffering of Christ, the judgment of God against those who oppose Him, and the pleas of His people for mercy in the face

*of oppression. We may use it to intercede for the lost, to praise
Jesus for His suffering, and to seek His help in our times of
need. Read Hebrews 12:3–13.*

To the Chief Musician. A Psalm of David.

Pray that God would strengthen His people against the oppression of men or spirits.

¹Do not keep silent,
O God of my praise!
²For the mouth of the wicked and the mouth of the
    deceitful
Have opened against me;
They have spoken against me with a lying tongue.
³They have also surrounded me with words of hatred,
And fought against me without a cause.
⁴In return for my love they are my accusers,
But I *give myself* to prayer.
⁵Thus they have rewarded me evil for good,
And hatred for my love.

Recall with gratitude the betrayal of Jesus, and pray for the lost, lest they come under the judgment of God.

⁶Set a wicked man over him,
And let an accuser stand at his right hand.
⁷When he is judged, let him be found guilty,
And let his prayer become sin.
⁸Let his days be few,
And let another take his office.
⁹Let his children be fatherless,
And his wife a widow.
¹⁰Let his children continually be vagabonds, and beg;
Let them seek *their bread* also from their desolate
    places.
¹¹Let the creditor seize all that he has,
And let strangers plunder his labor.

¹²Let there be none to extend mercy to him,
Nor let there be any to favor his fatherless children.
¹³Let his posterity be cut off,
And in the generation following let their name be
blotted out.

Pray that God would convict the wicked of their sin and turn their hearts to Him before they know His wrath.

¹⁴Let the iniquity of his fathers be remembered before
the LORD,
And let not the sin of his mother be blotted out.
¹⁵Let them be continually before the LORD,
That He may cut off the memory of them from the
earth;
¹⁶Because he did not remember to show mercy,
But persecuted the poor and needy man,
That he might even slay the broken in heart.
¹⁷As he loved cursing, so let it come to him;
As he did not delight in blessing, so let it be far from
him.
¹⁸As he clothed himself with cursing as with his
garment,
So let it enter his body like water,
And like oil into his bones.
¹⁹Let it be to him like the garment which covers him,
And for a belt with which he girds himself
continually.
²⁰*Let* this *be* the LORD's reward to my accusers,
And to those who speak evil against my person.

Seek the mercy of God for strength in the face of opposition.

²¹But You, O GOD the Lord,
Deal with me for Your name's sake;
Because Your mercy *is* good, deliver me.

²²For I *am* poor and needy,
And my heart is wounded within me.
²³I am gone like a shadow when it lengthens;
I am shaken off like a locust.
²⁴My knees are weak through fasting,
And my flesh is feeble from lack of fatness.
²⁵I also have become a reproach to them;
When they look at me, they shake their heads.

²⁶Help me, O LORD my God!
Oh, save me according to Your mercy,
²⁷That they may know that this *is* Your hand—
That You, LORD, have done it!
²⁸Let them curse, but You bless;
When they arise, they shall be ashamed,
But let Your servant rejoice.
²⁹Let my accusers be clothed with shame,
And let them cover themselves with their own
    disgrace as with a mantle.

Praise the Lord, who saves His oppressed people.

³⁰I will greatly praise the LORD with my mouth;
Yes, I will praise Him among the multitude.
³¹For He shall stand at the right hand of the poor,
To save *him* from those who condemn him.

Psalm 110

This royal psalm foresees the exaltation of Christ and His coming in judgment. Praise Him, our Lord and King, who ever lives to make intercession for us. Read Hebrews 7:1–25.

A Psalm of David.

Praise Christ for His sovereign rule, and pray that it might advance among the nations of the earth.

¹The LORD said to my Lord,
"Sit at My right hand,
Till I make Your enemies Your footstool."
²The LORD shall send the rod of Your strength out of
     Zion.
Rule in the midst of Your enemies!

Pray that God would mobilize His people for service, as Christ intercedes for them.

³Your people *shall be* volunteers
In the day of Your power;
In the beauties of holiness, from the womb of the
     morning.
You have the dew of Your youth.
⁴The LORD has sworn
And will not relent,
"You *are* a priest forever
According to the order of Melchizedek."

In the light of Jesus' return in judgment, pray for the salvation of the nations.

⁵The Lord *is* at Your right hand;
He shall execute kings in the day of His wrath.
⁶He shall judge among the nations,
He shall fill *the places* with dead bodies,
He shall execute the heads of many countries.
⁷He shall drink of the brook by the wayside;
Therefore He shall lift up the head.

Psalm 111

This psalm of praise can lead us to rejoice in the works of the Lord and to renew our commitment to Him. Read John 1:1–12.

Praise the Lord for His many wonderful works and for His faithfulness.

¹Praise the LORD!

I will praise the LORD with *my* whole heart,
In the assembly of the upright and *in* the
  congregation.

²The works of the LORD *are* great,
Studied by all who have pleasure in them.
³His work *is* honorable and glorious,
And His righteousness endures forever.
⁴He has made His wonderful works to be
  remembered;
The LORD *is* gracious and full of compassion.
⁵He has given food to those who fear Him;
He will ever be mindful of His covenant.
⁶He has declared to His people the power of His
  works,
In giving them the heritage of the nations.

Praise God for His Word, and resolve to submit to it for the wisdom of God.

⁷The works of His hands *are* verity and justice;
All His precepts *are* sure.
⁸They stand fast forever and ever,
And are done in truth and uprightness.
⁹He has sent redemption to His people;
He has commanded His covenant forever;
Holy and awesome *is* His name.

¹⁰The fear of the L<small>ORD</small> *is* the beginning of wisdom;
A good understanding have all those who do *His*
   commandments.
His praise endures forever.

Psalm 112

Use this wisdom psalm as the psalmist himself did, to seek God's blessings for yourself and all those who fear the Lord. Read Galatians 6:1–10.

Praise God for His blessings, and ask His help to delight in His Word.

¹Praise the L<small>ORD</small>!

Blessed *is* the man *who* fears the L<small>ORD</small>,
Who delights greatly in His commandments.

Seek the blessings of God for yourself and all those who fear Him.

²His descendants will be mighty on earth;
The generation of the upright will be blessed.
³Wealth and riches *will be* in his house,
And his righteousness endures forever.
⁴Unto the upright there arises light in the darkness;
He is gracious, and full of compassion, and righteous.
⁵A good man deals graciously and lends;
He will guide his affairs with discretion.
⁶Surely he will never be shaken;
The righteous will be in everlasting remembrance.
⁷He will not be afraid of evil tidings;
His heart is steadfast, trusting in the L<small>ORD</small>.

⁸His heart *is* established;
He will not be afraid,
Until he sees *his desire* upon his enemies.

Pray that God would use His people to minister His grace and to defeat His enemies.

⁹He has dispersed abroad,
He has given to the poor;
His righteousness endures forever;
His horn will be exalted with honor.
¹⁰The wicked will see *it* and be grieved;
He will gnash his teeth and melt away;
The desire of the wicked shall perish.

Psalm 113

This psalm praises the Lord for His majesty and compassion, and we may use it in just this way. Read Ephesians 3:14–19.

Praise the majestic greatness of God.

¹Praise the LORD!

Praise, O servants of the LORD,
Praise the name of the LORD!
²Blessed be the name of the LORD
From this time forth and forevermore!
³From the rising of the sun to its going down
The LORD's name *is* to be praised.

⁴The LORD is high above all nations,
And His glory above the heavens.

Praise Him who condescends to care for us in our weakness.

⁵Who *is* like the Lᴏʀᴅ our God,
Who dwells on high,
⁶Who humbles Himself to behold
The things that are in the heavens and in the earth?

⁷He raises the poor out of the dust,
And lifts the needy out of the ash heap,
⁸That He may seat *him* with princes—
With the princes of His people.
⁹He grants the barren woman a home,
Like a joyful mother of children.

Praise the Lᴏʀᴅ!

Psalm 114

This is a psalm of testimony, declaring with confidence the dwelling of God with His people. Use it to praise the Lord for His promise to be with us always and for all His mighty works on our behalf. Read Matthew 28:18–20.

Praise the Lord, who has come to dwell in our midst by His Spirit.

¹When Israel went out of Egypt,
The house of Jacob from a people of strange
    language,
²Judah became His sanctuary,
And Israel His dominion.

Recall God's might in delivering Israel, and meditate on His many wondrous works for you.

³The sea saw *it* and fled;
Jordan turned back.
⁴The mountains skipped like rams,
The little hills like lambs.
⁵What ails you, O sea, that you fled?
O Jordan, *that* you turned back?
⁶O mountains, *that* you skipped like rams?
O little hills, like lambs?

⁷Tremble, O earth, at the presence of the Lord,
At the presence of the God of Jacob,
⁸Who turned the rock *into* a pool of water,
The flint into a fountain of waters.

Psalm 115

This is a psalm of testimony, calling Israel to turn from idols and to trust the Lord, and holding out the promise of blessing for His people. Use it to pray for God's people today, that they would trust in Him and not fall into idolatrous ways. Read 1 John 5:13–21.

Glorify God for His sovereign mercy, truth, and greatness.

¹Not unto us, O LORD, not unto us,
But to Your name give glory,
Because of Your mercy
And because of Your truth.
²Why should the Gentiles say,
"Where now *is* their God?"

³But our God *is* in heaven;
He does whatever He pleases.

Pray that God's people would not give in to the temptation of idols.

⁴Their idols *are* silver and gold,
The work of men's hands.
⁵They have mouths, but they do not speak;
Eyes they have, but they do not see;
⁶They have ears, but they do not hear;
Noses they have, but they do not smell;
⁷They have hands, but they do not handle;
Feet they have, but they do not walk;
Nor do they mutter through their throat.
⁸Those who make them are like them;
So is everyone who trusts in them.

Pray that God's people may trust in Him alone.

⁹O Israel, trust in the LORD;
He *is* their help and their shield.
¹⁰O house of Aaron, trust in the LORD;
He *is* their help and their shield.
¹¹You who fear the LORD, trust in the LORD;
He *is* their help and their shield.

Recall, and claim again, the many blessings of God.

¹²The LORD has been mindful of *us;*
He will bless us;
He will bless the house of Israel;
He will bless the house of Aaron.
¹³He will bless those who fear the LORD,
Both small and great.

¹⁴May the LORD give you increase more and more,
You and your children.

¹⁵*May* you *be* blessed by the LORD,
Who made heaven and earth.

Praise God, who gives great blessings to His people.

¹⁶The heaven, *even* the heavens, *are* the LORD's;
But the earth He has given to the children of men.
¹⁷The dead do not praise the LORD,
Nor any who go down into silence.
¹⁸But we will bless the LORD
From this time forth and forevermore.

Praise the LORD!

Psalm 116

This is a psalm of testimony. Use it to praise God for the times He has sustained you through trial, or to prepare you for temptations and trials to come. Read 2 Timothy 4:9–18.

Declare your love for the Lord, who hears your prayers in time of need.

¹I love the LORD, because He has heard
My voice *and* my supplications.
²Because He has inclined His ear to me,
Therefore I will call *upon Him* as long as I live.

Praise God, who has redeemed you from the grave.

³The pains of death encompassed me,
And the pangs of Sheol laid hold of me;
I found trouble and sorrow.

⁴Then I called upon the name of the Lᴏʀᴅ:
"O Lᴏʀᴅ, I implore You, deliver my soul!"

Praise God for His grace and mercy, and for delivering you as you trust in Him.

⁵Gracious *is* the Lᴏʀᴅ, and righteous;
Yes, our God *is* merciful.
⁶The Lᴏʀᴅ preserves the simple;
I was brought low, and He saved me.
⁷Return to your rest, O my soul,
For the Lᴏʀᴅ has dealt bountifully with you.

⁸For You have delivered my soul from death,
My eyes from tears,
And my feet from falling.
⁹I will walk before the Lᴏʀᴅ
In the land of the living.
¹⁰I believed, therefore I spoke,
"I am greatly afflicted."
¹¹I said in my haste,
"All men *are* liars."

Seek to know more of God's salvation, and seek His strength to fulfill all your vows.

¹²What shall I render to the Lᴏʀᴅ
For all His benefits toward me?
¹³I will take up the cup of salvation,
And call upon the name of the Lᴏʀᴅ.
¹⁴I will pay my vows to the Lᴏʀᴅ
Now in the presence of all His people.

¹⁵Precious in the sight of the Lᴏʀᴅ
Is the death of His saints.

¹⁶O LORD, truly I *am* Your servant;
I *am* Your servant, the son of Your maidservant;
You have loosed my bonds.
¹⁷I will offer to You the sacrifice of thanksgiving,
And will call upon the name of the LORD.

¹⁸I will pay my vows to the LORD
Now in the presence of all His people,
¹⁹In the courts of the LORD's house,
In the midst of you, O Jerusalem.

Praise the LORD!

Psalm 117

Use this very brief psalm of praise to exalt the Lord. Seek the increase of His praise throughout the earth. Read Philippians 2:5–11.

Pray that God would lead more peoples to praise Him for His mercy, truth, and love.

¹Oh, praise the LORD, all you Gentiles!
Laud Him, all you peoples!
²For His merciful kindness is great toward us,
And the truth of the LORD *endures* forever.

Praise the LORD!

Psalm 118

God is praised and magnified for His mercy in saving His people. Use this psalm on Sunday afternoons, as it brings together so many of the events of Christ's passion and leads us to praise Him for His saving work. Read Matthew 21:4–11, 42–46.

Praise God for His mercy and goodness to His people.

¹Oh, give thanks to the LORD, for *He is* good!
Because His mercy *endures* forever.

²Let Israel now say,
"His mercy *endures* forever."
³Let the house of Aaron now say,
"His mercy *endures* forever."
⁴Let those who fear the LORD now say,
"His mercy *endures* forever."

Meditate on Jesus' suffering, and praise Him for His strength and faith in bearing God's wrath against us.

⁵I called on the LORD in distress;
The LORD answered me *and set me* in a broad place.
⁶The LORD *is* on my side;
I will not fear.
What can man do to me?
⁷The LORD is for me among those who help me;
Therefore I shall see *my desire* on those who hate me.
⁸*It is* better to trust in the LORD
Than to put confidence in man.
⁹*It is* better to trust in the LORD
Than to put confidence in princes.

¹⁰All nations surrounded me,
But in the name of the LORD I will destroy them.
¹¹They surrounded me,
Yes, they surrounded me;
But in the name of the LORD I will destroy them.
¹²They surrounded me like bees;
They were quenched like a fire of thorns;
For in the name of the LORD I will destroy them.
¹³You pushed me violently, that I might fall,
But the LORD helped me.
¹⁴The LORD *is* my strength and song,
And He has become my salvation.

Praise God that His right hand, our Lord Jesus, has accomplished our salvation.

¹⁵The voice of rejoicing and salvation
Is in the tents of the righteous;
The right hand of the LORD does valiantly.
¹⁶The right hand of the LORD is exalted;
The right hand of the LORD does valiantly.
¹⁷I shall not die, but live,
And declare the works of the LORD.
¹⁸The LORD has chastened me severely,
But He has not given me over to death.

¹⁹Open to me the gates of righteousness;
I will go through them,
And I will praise the LORD.
²⁰This is the gate of the LORD,
Through which the righteous shall enter.

²¹I will praise You,
For You have answered me,
And have become my salvation.

Pray for the salvation of the lost, that they might not stumble on the cornerstone, which is Jesus.

²²The stone *which* the builders rejected
Has become the chief cornerstone.
²³This was the LORD's doing;
It *is* marvelous in our eyes.
²⁴This *is* the day *which* the LORD has made;
We will rejoice and be glad in it.

²⁵Save now, I pray, O LORD;
O LORD, I pray, send now prosperity.
²⁶Blessed *is* he who comes in the name of the LORD!
We have blessed you from the house of the LORD.
²⁷God *is* the LORD,
And He has given us light;
Bind the sacrifice with cords to the horns of the altar.
²⁸You *are* my God, and I will praise You;
You are my God, I will exalt You.

²⁹Oh, give thanks to the LORD, for *He is* good!
For His mercy *endures* forever.

Psalm 119

This beloved wisdom psalm celebrates the many benefits of God's Word. You can use a portion of it before the reading and study of Scripture each day. Read 2 Timothy 3:15–17; Hebrews 4:12.

ALEPH

Ask the Lord to help you keep His Word and to bless you as you do.

¹Blessed *are* the undefiled in the way,
Who walk in the law of the LORD!

²Blessed *are* those who keep His testimonies,
Who seek Him with the whole heart!
³They also do no iniquity;
They walk in His ways.
⁴You have commanded *us*
To keep Your precepts diligently.
⁵Oh, that my ways were directed
To keep Your statutes!
⁶Then I would not be ashamed,
When I look into all Your commandments.
⁷I will praise You with uprightness of heart,
When I learn Your righteous judgments.
⁸I will keep Your statutes;
Oh, do not forsake me utterly!

BETH

**Ask the Lord to enable you to delight in and obey
His Word.**

⁹How can a young man cleanse his way?
By taking heed according to Your word.
¹⁰With my whole heart I have sought You;
Oh, let me not wander from Your commandments!
¹¹Your word I have hidden in my heart,
That I might not sin against You.
¹²Blessed *are* You, O Lᴏʀᴅ!
Teach me Your statutes.
¹³With my lips I have declared
All the judgments of Your mouth.
¹⁴I have rejoiced in the way of Your testimonies,
As *much as* in all riches.
¹⁵I will meditate on Your precepts,
And contemplate Your ways.
¹⁶I will delight myself in Your statutes;
I will not forget Your word.

GIMEL

Ask the Lord to make His Word clear to you, that you might keep it.

¹⁷Deal bountifully with Your servant,
That I may live and keep Your word.
¹⁸Open my eyes, that I may see
Wondrous things from Your law.
¹⁹I *am* a stranger in the earth;
Do not hide Your commandments from me.
²⁰My soul breaks with longing
For Your judgments at all times.
²¹You rebuke the proud—the cursed,
Who stray from Your commandments.
²²Remove from me reproach and contempt,
For I have kept Your testimonies.
²³Princes also sit *and* speak against me,
But Your servant meditates on Your statutes.
²⁴Your testimonies also *are* my delight
And my counselors.

DALETH

Pray that God would revive and strengthen you by His Word.

²⁵My soul clings to the dust;
Revive me according to Your word.
²⁶I have declared my ways, and You answered me;
Teach me Your statutes.
²⁷Make me understand the way of Your precepts;
So shall I meditate on Your wondrous works.
²⁸My soul melts from heaviness;
Strengthen me according to Your word.
²⁹Remove from me the way of lying,
And grant me Your law graciously.
³⁰I have chosen the way of truth;
Your judgments I have laid *before me*.

³¹I cling to Your testimonies;
O Lord, do not put me to shame!
³²I will run in the way of Your commandments,
For You enlarge my heart.

HE

Pray for revival and a heart devoted to keeping God's Word.

³³Teach me, O Lord, the way of Your statutes,
And I shall keep it *to* the end.
³⁴Give me understanding, and I shall keep Your law;
Indeed, I shall observe it with *my* whole heart.
³⁵Make me walk in the path of Your commandments,
For I delight in it.
³⁶Incline my heart to Your testimonies,
And not to covetousness.
³⁷Turn away my eyes from looking at worthless
     things,
And revive me in Your way.
³⁸Establish Your word to Your servant,
Who *is devoted* to fearing You.
³⁹Turn away my reproach which I dread,
For Your judgments *are* good.
⁴⁰Behold, I long for Your precepts;
Revive me in Your righteousness.

WAW

Pray that you might delight and stand firm in the Word of God.

⁴¹Let Your mercies come also to me, O Lord—
Your salvation according to Your word.
⁴²So shall I have an answer for him who reproaches
     me,
For I trust in Your word.
⁴³And take not the word of truth utterly out of my
     mouth,
For I have hoped in Your ordinances.

[44]So shall I keep Your law continually,
Forever and ever.
[45]And I will walk at liberty,
For I seek Your precepts.
[46]I will speak of Your testimonies also before kings,
And will not be ashamed.
[47]And I will delight myself in Your commandments,
Which I love.
[48]My hands also I will lift up to Your commandments,
Which I love,
And I will meditate on Your statutes.

ZAYIN

Pray that God would comfort you by His Word.

[49]Remember the word to Your servant,
Upon which You have caused me to hope.
[50]This *is* my comfort in my affliction,
For Your word has given me life.
[51]The proud have me in great derision,
Yet I do not turn aside from Your law.
[52]I remembered Your judgments of old, O LORD,
And have comforted myself.
[53]Indignation has taken hold of me
Because of the wicked, who forsake Your law.
[54]Your statutes have been my songs
In the house of my pilgrimage.
[55]I remember Your name in the night, O LORD,
And I keep Your law.
[56]This has become mine,
Because I kept Your precepts.

HETH

Seek the mercy and favor of the Lord, that you might fear Him and keep His Word.

[57]*You are* my portion, O LORD;
I have said that I would keep Your words.

58I entreated Your favor with *my* whole heart;
Be merciful to me according to Your word.
59I thought about my ways,
And turned my feet to Your testimonies.
60I made haste, and did not delay
To keep Your commandments.
61The cords of the wicked have bound me,
But I have not forgotten Your law.
62At midnight I will rise to give thanks to You,
Because of Your righteous judgments.
63I *am* a companion of all *those* who fear You,
And of those who keep Your precepts.
64The earth, O Lord, is full of Your mercy;
Teach me Your statutes.

TETH

**Pray that God's Word would strengthen you in
times of affliction or temptation.**

65You have dealt well with Your servant,
O Lord, according to Your word.
66Teach me good judgment and knowledge,
For I believe Your commandments.
67Before I was afflicted I went astray,
But now I keep Your word.
68You *are* good, and do good;
Teach me Your statutes.
69The proud have forged a lie against me,
But I will keep Your precepts with *my* whole heart.
70Their heart is as fat as grease,
But I delight in Your law.
71*It is* good for me that I have been afflicted,
That I may learn Your statutes.
72The law of Your mouth is better to me
Than thousands of *shekels of* gold and silver.

Seek mercy, that God may comfort you by His Word in times of trial.

⁷³Your hands have made me and fashioned me;
Give me understanding, that I may learn Your
    commandments.
⁷⁴Those who fear You will be glad when they see me,
Because I have hoped in Your word.
⁷⁵I know, O Lᴏʀᴅ, that Your judgments *are* right,
And that in faithfulness You have afflicted me.
⁷⁶Let, I pray, Your merciful kindness be for my
    comfort,
According to Your word to Your servant.
⁷⁷Let Your tender mercies come to me, that I may live;
For Your law *is* my delight.
⁷⁸Let the proud be ashamed,
For they treat me wrongfully with falsehood;
But I will meditate on Your precepts.
⁷⁹Let those who fear You turn to me,
Those who know Your testimonies.
⁸⁰Let my heart be blameless regarding Your statutes,
That I may not be ashamed.

Ask the Lord to strengthen you by His Word against those who torment you.

⁸¹My soul faints for Your salvation,
But I hope in Your word.
⁸²My eyes fail *from seeking* Your word,
Saying, "When will You comfort me?"
⁸³For I have become like a wineskin in smoke,
Yet I do not forget Your statutes.
⁸⁴How many *are* the days of Your servant?
When will You execute judgment on those who
    persecute me?

[85]The proud have dug pits for me,
Which *is* not according to Your law.
[86]All Your commandments *are* faithful;
They persecute me wrongfully;
Help me!
[87]They almost made an end of me on earth,
But I did not forsake Your precepts.
[88]Revive me according to Your lovingkindness,
So that I may keep the testimony of Your mouth.

LAMED

Praise God for the sustaining power of His Word.

[89]Forever, O LORD,
Your word is settled in heaven.
[90]Your faithfulness *endures* to all generations;
You established the earth, and it abides.
[91]They continue this day according to Your
    ordinances,
For all *are* Your servants.
[92]Unless Your law *had been* my delight,
I would then have perished in my affliction.
[93]I will never forget Your precepts,
For by them You have given me life.
[94]I *am* Yours, save me;
For I have sought Your precepts.
[95]The wicked wait for me to destroy me,
But I will consider Your testimonies.
[96]I have seen the consummation of all perfection,
But Your commandment *is* exceedingly broad.

MEM

**Pray that you may cherish God's Word more and
more, and meditate on it daily.**

[97]Oh, how I love Your law!
It *is* my meditation all the day.

[98]You, through Your commandments, make me wiser
than my enemies;
For they *are* ever with me.
[99]I have more understanding than all my teachers,
For Your testimonies *are* my meditation.
[100]I understand more than the ancients,
Because I keep Your precepts.
[101]I have restrained my feet from every evil way,
That I may keep Your word.
[102]I have not departed from Your judgments,
For You Yourself have taught me.
[103]How sweet are Your words to my taste,
Sweeter than honey to my mouth!
[104]Through Your precepts I get understanding;
Therefore I hate every false way.

NUN

**Pray that God would guide, teach, and guard you
by His Word.**

[105]Your word *is* a lamp to my feet
And a light to my path.
[106]I have sworn and confirmed
That I will keep Your righteous judgments.
[107]I am afflicted very much;
Revive me, O LORD, according to Your word.
[108]Accept, I pray, the freewill offerings of my mouth,
O LORD,
And teach me Your judgments.
[109]My life *is* continually in my hand,
Yet I do not forget Your law.
[110]The wicked have laid a snare for me,
Yet I have not strayed from Your precepts.
[111]Your testimonies I have taken as a heritage forever,
For they *are* the rejoicing of my heart.
[112]I have inclined my heart to perform Your statutes
Forever, to the very end.

SAMEK

Pray that God may keep you from evil and wickedness by His Word.

¹¹³I hate the double-minded,
But I love Your law.
¹¹⁴You *are* my hiding place and my shield;
I hope in Your word.
¹¹⁵Depart from me, you evildoers,
For I will keep the commandments of my God!
¹¹⁶Uphold me according to Your word, that I may live;
And do not let me be ashamed of my hope.
¹¹⁷Hold me up, and I shall be safe,
And I shall observe Your statutes continually.
¹¹⁸You reject all those who stray from Your statutes,
For their deceit *is* falsehood.
¹¹⁹You put away all the wicked of the earth *like* dross;
Therefore I love Your testimonies.
¹²⁰My flesh trembles for fear of You,
And I am afraid of Your judgments.

AYIN

Pray for understanding of God's Word and that He might strengthen you against all hopelessness and oppression.

¹²¹I have done justice and righteousness;
Do not leave me to my oppressors.
¹²²Be surety for Your servant for good;
Do not let the proud oppress me.
¹²³My eyes fail *from seeking* Your salvation
And Your righteous word.
¹²⁴Deal with Your servant according to Your mercy,
And teach me Your statutes.
¹²⁵I *am* Your servant;
Give me understanding,
That I may know Your testimonies.

¹²⁶*It is* time for *You* to act, O LORD,
For they have regarded Your law as void.
¹²⁷Therefore I love Your commandments
More than gold, yes, than fine gold!
¹²⁸Therefore all *Your* precepts *concerning* all *things*
I consider *to be* right;
I hate every false way.

PE

**Long for God's Word, and pray that He might
enlighten and guide you by it.**

¹²⁹Your testimonies are wonderful;
Therefore my soul keeps them.
¹³⁰The entrance of Your words gives light;
It gives understanding to the simple.
¹³¹I opened my mouth and panted,
For I longed for Your commandments.
¹³²Look upon me and be merciful to me,
As Your custom *is* toward those who love Your name.
¹³³Direct my steps by Your word,
And let no iniquity have dominion over me.
¹³⁴Redeem me from the oppression of man,
That I may keep Your precepts.
¹³⁵Make Your face shine upon Your servant,
And teach me Your statutes.
¹³⁶Rivers of water run down from my eyes,
Because *men* do not keep Your law.

TSADDE

**Pray that God would increase your love for and
delight in His Word.**

¹³⁷Righteous *are* You, O LORD,
And upright *are* Your judgments.
¹³⁸Your testimonies, *which* You have commanded,
Are righteous and very faithful.

¹³⁹My zeal has consumed me,
Because my enemies have forgotten Your words.
¹⁴⁰Your word *is* very pure;
Therefore Your servant loves it.
¹⁴¹I *am* small and despised,
Yet I do not forget Your precepts.
¹⁴²Your righteousness *is* an everlasting righteousness,
And Your law *is* truth.
¹⁴³Trouble and anguish have overtaken me,
Yet Your commandments *are* my delights.
¹⁴⁴The righteousness of Your testimonies *is*
    everlasting;
Give me understanding, and I shall live.

QOPH

Hope in God's Word, meditate on it, and resolve to obey as God leads.

¹⁴⁵I cry out with my whole heart;
Hear me, O LORD!
I will keep Your statutes.
¹⁴⁶I cry out to You;
Save me, and I will keep Your testimonies.
¹⁴⁷I rise before the dawning of the morning,
And cry for help; ·
I hope in Your word.
¹⁴⁸My eyes are awake through the *night* watches,
That I may meditate on Your word.
¹⁴⁹Hear my voice according to Your lovingkindness;
O LORD, revive me according to Your justice.
¹⁵⁰They draw near who follow after wickedness;
They are far from Your law.
¹⁵¹You *are* near, O LORD,
And all Your commandments are truth.
¹⁵²Concerning Your testimonies,
I have known of old that You have founded them
    forever.

RESH

Seek God's reviving grace as you read and study His Word.

¹⁵³Consider my affliction and deliver me,
For I do not forget Your law.
¹⁵⁴Plead my cause and redeem me;
Revive me according to Your word.
¹⁵⁵Salvation *is* far from the wicked,
For they do not seek Your statutes.
¹⁵⁶Great *are* Your tender mercies, O LORD;
Revive me according to Your judgments.
¹⁵⁷Many *are* my persecutors and my enemies,
Yet I do not turn from Your testimonies.
¹⁵⁸I see the treacherous, and am disgusted,
Because they do not keep Your word.
¹⁵⁹Consider how I love Your precepts;
Revive me, O LORD, according to Your
    lovingkindness.
¹⁶⁰The entirety of Your word *is* truth,
And every one of Your righteous judgments *endures*
    forever.

SHIN

Rejoice in the Word of God, and pray that He might increase your love for His truth.

¹⁶¹Princes persecute me without a cause,
But my heart stands in awe of Your word.
¹⁶²I rejoice at Your word
As one who finds great treasure.
¹⁶³I hate and abhor lying,
But I love Your law.
¹⁶⁴Seven times a day I praise You,
Because of Your righteous judgments.
¹⁶⁵Great peace have those who love Your law,
And nothing causes them to stumble.

¹⁶⁶LORD, I hope for Your salvation,
And I do Your commandments.
¹⁶⁷My soul keeps Your testimonies,
And I love them exceedingly.
¹⁶⁸I keep Your precepts and Your testimonies,
For all my ways *are* before You.

TAU

**Seek understanding and help from God's Word;
delight in it, and praise Him.**

¹⁶⁹Let my cry come before You, O LORD;
Give me understanding according to Your word.
¹⁷⁰Let my supplication come before You;
Deliver me according to Your word.
¹⁷¹My lips shall utter praise,
For You teach me Your statutes.
¹⁷²My tongue shall speak of Your word,
For all Your commandments *are* righteousness.
¹⁷³Let Your hand become my help,
For I have chosen Your precepts.
¹⁷⁴I long for Your salvation, O LORD,
And Your law *is* my delight.
¹⁷⁵Let my soul live, and it shall praise You;
And let Your judgments help me.
¹⁷⁶I have gone astray like a lost sheep;
Seek Your servant,
For I do not forget Your commandments.

Psalm 120

Use this psalm of complaint to seek the peace of Jesus in the midst of all adversity. Read Philippians 4:6–7.

A Song of Ascents.

Cry out to God to preserve you from deceiving men and spirits.

> ¹In my distress I cried to the LORD,
> And He heard me.
> ²Deliver my soul, O LORD, from lying lips
> *And* from a deceitful tongue.

Resist the devil and all foes who would alarm or deceive you or rob you of your peace. Rest in the Lord.

> ³What shall be given to you,
> Or what shall be done to you,
> You false tongue?
> ⁴Sharp arrows of the warrior,
> With coals of the broom tree!
>
> ⁵Woe is me, that I sojourn in Meshech,
> *That* I dwell among the tents of Kedar!
> ⁶My soul has dwelt too long
> With one who hates peace.
> ⁷I *am for* peace;
> But when I speak, they *are* for war.

Psalm 121

This psalm of testimony can prepare you for standing strong in the face of temptation and for serving the Lord each day. Read Ephesians 6:10–20.

A Song of Ascents.

Look to the Lord for the help you need each day.

¹I will lift up my eyes to the hills—
From whence comes my help?
²My help *comes* from the LORD,
Who made heaven and earth.

³He will not allow your foot to be moved;
He who keeps you will not slumber.
⁴Behold, He who keeps Israel
Shall neither slumber nor sleep.

Praise the Lord, and trust in Him who is your keeper and help.

⁵The LORD *is* your keeper;
The LORD *is* your shade at your right hand.
⁶The sun shall not strike you by day,
Nor the moon by night.
⁷The LORD shall preserve you from all evil;
He shall preserve your soul.
⁸The LORD shall preserve your going out and coming
  in
From this time forth, and even forevermore.

Psalm 122

Use this psalm of testimony to prepare for the worship of the Lord. Read John 4:21–24.

A Song of Ascents. Of David.

Pray that God will fill His people with joy and gratitude as they come to worship Him.

> [1]I was glad when they said to me,
> "Let us go into the house of the Lord."
> [2]Our feet have been standing
> Within your gates, O Jerusalem!
>
> [3]Jerusalem is built
> As a city that is compact together,
> [4]Where the tribes go up,
> The tribes of the Lord,
> To the Testimony of Israel,
> To give thanks to the name of the Lord.
> [5]For thrones are set there for judgment,
> The thrones of the house of David.

Pray that God's church may know His peace.

> [6]Pray for the peace of Jerusalem:
> "May they prosper who love you.
> [7]Peace be within your walls,
> Prosperity within your palaces."
> [8]For the sake of my brethren and companions,
> I will now say, "Peace *be* within you."
> [9]Because of the house of the Lord our God
> I will seek your good.

273

Psalm 123

This is a psalm of testimony. Use it to seek mercy and strength from the Lord to serve Him, even in the face of scorn and adversity. Read Acts 7:54–60.

A Song of Ascents.

Renew your commitment to serve the Lord by the power of His grace.

¹Unto You I lift up my eyes,
O You who dwell in the heavens.
²Behold, as the eyes of servants *look* to the hand of
their masters,
As the eyes of a maid to the hand of her mistress,
So our eyes *look* to the LORD our God,
Until He has mercy on us.

Seek mercy from God to persevere in the midst of a hostile age.

³Have mercy on us, O LORD, have mercy on us!
For we are exceedingly filled with contempt.
⁴Our soul is exceedingly filled
With the scorn of those who are at ease,
With the contempt of the proud.

Psalm 124

This is a psalm of testimony and praise. Use it to intercede for the persecuted church, and to pray for yourself in the face of temptations and trials. Read Hebrews 13:1–6.

A Song of Ascents. Of David.

Praise God, who stands with you and all believers in the face of adversity.

¹"If it had not been the LORD who was on our side,"
Let Israel now say—
²"If it had not been the LORD who was on our side,
When men rose up against us,
³Then they would have swallowed us alive,
When their wrath was kindled against us;
⁴Then the waters would have overwhelmed us,
The stream would have gone over our soul;
⁵Then the swollen waters
Would have gone over our soul."

Praise the Lord, and pray that He will deliver all His suffering people.

⁶Blessed *be* the LORD,
Who has not given us *as* prey to their teeth.
⁷Our soul has escaped as a bird from the snare of the
    fowlers;
The snare is broken, and we have escaped.
⁸Our help *is* in the name of the LORD,
Who made heaven and earth.

Psalm 125

*This psalm has elements of testimony, complaint, and impre-
cation as it seeks the Lord's help against the wicked. Use it
to pray that God would make His church stand firm against
all unrighteousness. Read Matthew 5:43–48.*

A Song of Ascents.

Praise the Lord for His surrounding grace and indwelling Spirit.

¹Those who trust in the LORD
Are like Mount Zion,
Which cannot be moved, *but* abides forever.
²As the mountains surround Jerusalem,
So the LORD surrounds His people
From this time forth and forever.

Pray that God would keep His people from all sin.

³For the scepter of wickedness shall not rest
On the land allotted to the righteous,
Lest the righteous reach out their hands to iniquity.

Seek the good of the Lord for those who love and follow Him.

⁴Do good, O LORD, to *those who are* good,
And to *those who are* upright in their hearts.

⁵As for such as turn aside to their crooked ways,
The LORD shall lead them away
With the workers of iniquity.

Peace *be* upon Israel!

Psalm 126

This is a psalm of praise anticipating the renewing grace of the Lord. Pray this psalm to seek revival for the church and renewal in our mission. Read Matthew 28:18–20.

A Song of Ascents.

Praise God for the many wonderful things He has done for you and all His people.

¹When the LORD brought back the captivity of Zion,
We were like those who dream.
²Then our mouth was filled with laughter,
And our tongue with singing.
Then they said among the nations,
"The LORD has done great things for them."
³The LORD has done great things for us,
Whereof we are glad.

Pray that God would revive His church and that it would take up its mission with greater zeal.

⁴Bring back our captivity, O LORD,
As the streams in the South.

⁵Those who sow in tears
Shall reap in joy.
⁶He who continually goes forth weeping,
Bearing seed for sowing,
Shall doubtless come again with rejoicing,
Bringing his sheaves *with him.*

Psalm 127

This psalm of testimony makes an abrupt change of focus in the middle. Use it to seek the blessings of the Lord on all your work and on the children of the church. Read Philippians 4:10–20.

A Song of Ascents. Of Solomon.

Pray that God would bless all your endeavors and guard you daily.

¹Unless the LORD builds the house,
They labor in vain who build it;
Unless the LORD guards the city,
The watchman stays awake in vain.
²*It is* vain for you to rise up early,
To sit up late,
To eat the bread of sorrows;
For so He gives His beloved sleep.

Pray for the children of the church, for their parents, and for those who teach and shape them.

³Behold, children *are* a heritage from the LORD,
The fruit of the womb *is His* reward.
⁴Like arrows in the hand of a warrior,
So *are* the children of one's youth.
⁵Happy *is* the man who has his quiver full of them;
They shall not be ashamed,
But shall speak with their enemies in the gate.

Psalm 128

*Use this testimony psalm to pray for yourself and others,
that the blessings of God would abide with them and their
families. Read Colossians 4:17–25.*

A Song of Ascents.

Pray that God would teach you to fear and follow Him.

¹Blessed *is* every one who fears the LORD,
Who walks in His ways.

Seek God's blessings on your work and family and on all who fear the Lord.

²When you eat the labor of your hands,
You *shall be* happy, and *it shall be* well with you.
³Your wife *shall be* like a fruitful vine
In the very heart of your house,
Your children like olive plants
All around your table.
⁴Behold, thus shall the man be blessed
Who fears the LORD.

⁵The LORD bless you out of Zion,
And may you see the good of Jerusalem
All the days of your life.
⁶Yes, may you see your children's children.

Peace *be* upon Israel!

Psalm 129

This psalm has elements of complaint and imprecation, seeking God's justice against those who oppress His people. Use it to pray for the persecuted church, or for strength to stand firm in spiritual warfare. Read Ephesians 6:1–20.

A Song of Ascents.

Praise the Lord, who preserves His people in the face of oppression.

[1]"Many a time they have afflicted me from my youth,"
Let Israel now say—
[2]"Many a time they have afflicted me from my youth;
Yet they have not prevailed against me.
[3]The plowers plowed on my back;
They made their furrows long."
[4]The LORD *is* righteous;
He has cut in pieces the cords of the wicked.

Pray that those who oppress the church might know the power of God against them.

[5]Let all those who hate Zion
Be put to shame and turned back.
[6]Let them be as the grass *on* the housetops,
Which withers before it grows up,
[7]With which the reaper does not fill his hand,
Nor he who binds sheaves, his arms.
[8]Neither let those who pass by them say,
"The blessing of the LORD *be* upon you;
We bless you in the name of the LORD!"

Psalm 130

Use this psalm of complaint and confession to seek the grace and mercy of the Lord for forgiveness of sins and help in times of need. Read Hebrews 4:14–16.

A Song of Ascents.

Confess your sins to the Lord, and bring your needs before Him.

¹Out of the depths I have cried to You, O LORD;
²Lord, hear my voice!
Let Your ears be attentive
To the voice of my supplications.

³If You, LORD, should mark iniquities,
O Lord, who could stand?
⁴But *there is* forgiveness with You,
That You may be feared.

Wait on the Lord, and hope in His Word; thank Him for the promise of redemption.

⁵I wait for the LORD, my soul waits,
And in His word I do hope.
⁶My soul *waits* for the Lord
More than those who watch for the morning—
Yes, more than those who watch for the morning.

⁷O Israel, hope in the LORD;
For with the LORD *there is* mercy,
And with Him *is* abundant redemption.
⁸And He shall redeem Israel
From all his iniquities.

Psalm 131

Use this psalm of testimony to review the Lord's calling on your life and to rest yourself in Him. Read Ephesians 5:15–21.

A Song of Ascents. Of David.

Review your calling in life. Ask the Lord to deliver you from any vain or self-serving ways or hopes.

> ¹LORD, my heart is not haughty,
> Nor my eyes lofty.
> Neither do I concern myself with great matters,
> Nor with things too profound for me.

Rest in the Lord, and hope in Him.

> ²Surely I have calmed and quieted my soul,
> Like a weaned child with his mother;
> Like a weaned child *is* my soul within me.
>
> ³O Israel, hope in the LORD
> From this time forth and forever.

Psalm 132

This is a psalm of testimony. Use it to praise the Lord for ful-filling His covenant with David in the Lord Jesus Christ, and for including you in His promises. Read 2 Corinthians 1:19–21.

A Song of Ascents.

Praise God for the faith of David.

¹L<small>ORD</small>, remember David
And all his afflictions;
²How he swore to the L<small>ORD</small>,
And vowed to the Mighty *God* of Jacob;
³"Surely I will not go into the chamber of my house,
Or go up to the comfort of my bed;
⁴I will not give sleep to my eyes
Or slumber to my eyelids,
⁵Until I find a place for the L<small>ORD</small>,
A dwelling place for the Mighty *God* of Jacob."

Call upon the Lord to lead His church to seek the fullness of His covenant.

⁶Behold, we heard of it in Ephrathah;
We found it in the fields of the woods.
⁷Let us go into His tabernacle;
Let us worship at His footstool.
⁸Arise, O L<small>ORD</small>, to Your resting place,
You and the ark of Your strength.
⁹Let Your priests be clothed with righteousness,
And let Your saints shout for joy.

¹⁰For Your servant David's sake,
Do not turn away the face of Your Anointed.

Praise God for the promises of His covenant, which He has fulfilled in Christ. Seek His promises earnestly.

¹¹The L<small>ORD</small> has sworn *in* truth to David;
He will not turn from it;
"I will set upon your throne the fruit of your body.
¹²If your sons will keep My covenant
And my testimony which I shall teach them,

Their sons also shall sit upon your throne
   forevermore."

[13]For the LORD has chosen Zion;
He has desired *it* for His habitation:
[14]"This *is* My resting place forever;
Here I will dwell, for I have desired it.
[15]I will abundantly bless her provision;
I will satisfy her poor with bread.
[16]I will also clothe her priests with salvation,
And her saints shall shout aloud for joy.
[17]There I will make the horn of David grow;
I will prepare a lamp for My Anointed.
[18]His enemies I will clothe with shame,
But upon Himself His crown shall flourish."

Psalm 133

Use this psalm of testimony to seek unity among the churches of our Lord. Read John 17:21.

A Song of Ascents. Of David.

Ask God to help you see the beauty of unity. Seek it for His churches.

[1]Behold, how good and how pleasant *it is*
For brethren to dwell together in unity!

Recall how God's glory was revealed at Aaron's anointing, and seek the glory of the Lord for a unified church.

[2]*It is* like the precious oil upon the head,
Running down on the beard,

The beard of Aaron,
Running down on the edge of his garments.
³*It is* like the dew of Hermon,
Descending upon the mountains of Zion;
For there the LORD commanded the blessing—
Life forevermore.

Psalm 134

Use this psalm to intercede for those who serve the Lord in the church. Read 1 Timothy 2:1–2.

A Song of Ascents.

Pray for God's servants, that they might bless the Lord and serve Him faithfully.

¹Behold, bless the LORD,
All *you* servants of the LORD,
Who by night stand in the house of the LORD!
²Lift up your hands *in* the sanctuary,
And bless the LORD.

Pray that God would bless His faithful servants.

³The LORD who made heaven and earth
Bless you from Zion!

Psalm 135

This psalm of praise also contains elements of admonition. Use it to praise the Lord for His goodness and greatness and to ask Him to change the hearts of idolaters. Read Romans 1:18–32.

Praise the Lord, and pray that His praise might increase among His servants.

¹Praise the LORD!

Praise the name of the LORD;
Praise *Him*, O you servants of the LORD!
²You who stand in the house of the LORD,
In the courts of the house of our God,
³Praise the LORD, for the LORD *is* good;
Sing praises to His name, for *it is* pleasant.
⁴For the LORD has chosen Jacob for Himself,
Israel for His special treasure.

⁵For I know that the LORD *is* great,
And our Lord *is* above all gods.
⁶Whatever the LORD pleases He does,
In heaven and in earth,
In the seas and in all deep places.
⁷He causes the vapors to ascend from the ends of the
        earth;
He makes lightning for the rain;
He brings the wind out of His treasuries.

Praise God for His redeeming grace.

⁸He destroyed the firstborn of Egypt,
Both of man and beast.
⁹He sent signs and wonders into the midst of you, O
        Egypt,
Upon Pharaoh and all his servants.

¹⁰He defeated many nations
And slew mighty kings—
¹¹Sihon king of the Amorites,
Og king of Bashan,
And all the kingdoms of Canaan—
¹²And gave their land *as* a heritage,
A heritage to Israel His people.

¹³Your name, O LORD, *endures* forever,
Your fame, O LORD, throughout all generations.
¹⁴For the LORD will judge His people,
And He will have compassion on His servants.

Pray that idolaters of all kinds might see the foolishness of their ways; ask the Lord to protect you from idols.

¹⁵The idols of the nations *are* silver and gold,
The work of men's hands.
¹⁶They have mouths, but they do not speak;
Eyes they have, but they do not see;
¹⁷They have ears, but they do not hear;
Nor is there *any* breath in their mouths.
¹⁸Those who make them are like them;
So is everyone who trusts in them.

Pray that praise to God might increase among His people.

¹⁹Bless the LORD, O house of Israel!
Bless the LORD, O house of Aaron!
²⁰Bless the LORD, O house of Levi!
You who fear the LORD, bless the LORD!
²¹Blessed be the LORD out of Zion,
Who dwells in Jerusalem!

Praise the LORD!

Psalm 136

This is a psalm of glorious thanksgiving for God's enduring mercy. Its use is obvious: rejoice in the Lord. Read Revelation 4:8–11.

Thank God for His mighty work of creation.

¹Oh, give thanks to the LORD, for *He is* good!
   For His mercy *endures* forever.
²Oh, give thanks to the God of gods!
   For His mercy *endures* forever.
³Oh, give thanks to the Lord of lords!
   For His mercy *endures* forever:

⁴To Him alone who does great wonders,
   For His mercy *endures* forever;
⁵To Him who by wisdom made the heavens,
   For His mercy *endures* forever;
⁶To Him who laid out the earth above the waters,
   For His mercy *endures* forever;
⁷To Him who made the great lights,
   For His mercy *endures* forever—
⁸The sun to rule by day,
   For His mercy *endures* forever;
⁹The moon and stars to rule by night,
   For His mercy *endures* forever.

Thank God for His mighty work of redemption.

¹⁰To Him who struck Egypt in their firstborn,
   For His mercy *endures* forever;
¹¹And brought out Israel from among them,
   For His mercy *endures* forever;
¹²With a strong hand, and an outstretched arm,
   For His mercy *endures* forever;
¹³To Him who divided the Red Sea in two,
   For His mercy *endures* forever;

[14]And made Israel pass through the midst of it,
    For His mercy *endures* forever;
[15]But overthrew Pharaoh and his army in the Red Sea,
    For His mercy *endures* forever;
[16]To Him who led His people through the wilderness,
    For His mercy *endures* forever;
[17]To Him who struck down great kings,
    For His mercy *endures* forever;
[18]And slew famous kings,
    For His mercy *endures* forever—
[19]Sihon king of the Amorites,
    For His mercy *endures* forever;
[20]And Og king of Bashan,
    For His mercy *endures* forever—
[21]And gave their land as a heritage,
    For His mercy *endures* forever;
[22]A heritage to Israel His servant,
    For His mercy *endures* forever.

Thank God for His providential care for His people.

[23]Who remembered us in our lowly state,
    For His mercy *endures* forever;
[24]And rescued us from our enemies,
    For His mercy *endures* forever;
[25]Who gives food to all flesh,
    For His mercy *endures* forever.

[26]Oh, give thanks to the God of heaven!
    For His mercy *endures* forever.

Psalm 137

This psalm of imprecation and complaint is perhaps the most difficult of all to pray. Use it to seek God's help in spiritual warfare and to ask that His hand would be against the enemies of God's people. Read Revelation 6:9–17.

Lament the captivity of God's people to anything that robs us of our joy in the Lord.

¹By the rivers of Babylon,
There we sat down, yea, we wept
When we remembered Zion.
²We hung our harps
Upon the willows in the midst of it.
³For there those who carried us away captive
 required of us a song
And those who plundered us *required of us* mirth,
Saying, "Sing us *one* of the songs of Zion!"

Meditate on God's beautiful plan for His church, and how far short of it we fall. Pray to see the church revived.

⁴How shall we sing the LORD's song
In a foreign land?
⁵If I forget you, O Jerusalem,
Let my right hand forget *her skill!*
⁶If I do not remember you,
Let my tongue cling to the roof of my mouth—
If I do not exalt Jerusalem
Above my chief joy.

Seek the mercy and justice of God against the enemies of His people.

⁷Remember, O LORD, against the sons of Edom
The day of Jerusalem,

Who said, "Raze *it,* raze *it,*
To its very foundation!"
⁸O daughter of Babylon, who are to be destroyed,
Happy *shall he be* who repays you as you have served
    us!
⁹Happy *shall he be* who takes and dashes
Your little ones against the rock.

Psalm 138

This is a psalm of praise to God for His greatness, compassion, and justice. Use it to rejoice in Him for His care for His people. Read Ephesians 2:19–22.

A Psalm of David.

Praise the Lord for His lovingkindness toward you, and for His Word.

¹I will praise You with my whole heart;
Before the gods I will sing praises to You.
²I will worship toward Your holy temple,
And praise Your name
For Your lovingkindness and Your truth;
For You have magnified Your word above all Your
    name.
³In the day when I cried out, You answered me,
And made me bold *with* strength in my soul.

Praise God for His greatness and compassion.

⁴All the kings of the earth shall praise You, O Lᴏʀᴅ,
When they hear the words of Your mouth.
⁵Yes, they shall sing of the ways of the Lᴏʀᴅ,
For great *is* the glory of the Lᴏʀᴅ.

⁶Though the LORD *is* on high,
Yet He regards the lowly;
But the proud He knows from afar.

Praise God for His care for you and for your salvation.

⁷Though I walk in the midst of trouble, You will
  revive me;
You will stretch out Your hand
Against the wrath of my enemies,
And Your right hand will save me.
⁸The LORD will perfect *that which* concerns me;
Your mercy, O LORD, *endures* forever;
Do not forsake the works of Your hands.

Psalm 139

This psalm of praise testifies of the greatness of God and His constant care for His people. Use it to praise God for His great wisdom and His Spirit. Read John 16:5–15.

For the Chief Musician. A Psalm of David.

Praise God for His infinite wisdom and grace.

¹O LORD, You have searched me and known *me.*
²You know my sitting down and my rising up;
You understand my thought afar off.
³You comprehend my path and my lying down,
And are acquainted with all my ways.
⁴For *there* is not a word on my tongue,
But behold, O LORD, You know it altogether.
⁵You have hedged me behind and before,
And laid Your hand upon me.

⁶*Such* knowledge *is* too wonderful for me;
It is high, I cannot *attain* it.

Praise the Lord for His Spirit, who is with us always.

⁷Where can I go from Your Spirit?
Or where can I flee from Your presence?
⁸If I ascend into heaven, You *are* there;
If I make my bed in hell, behold, You *are there.*
⁹*If* I take the wings of the morning,
And dwell in the uttermost parts of the sea,
¹⁰Even there Your hand shall lead me,
And Your right hand shall hold me.
¹¹If I say, "Surely the darkness shall fall on me,"
Even the night shall be light about me.
¹²Indeed, the darkness shall not hide from You,
But the night shines as the day;
The darkness and the light *are* both alike *to You.*

Praise God for His care in making you and in preparing the days of your life.

¹³For You have formed my inward parts;
You have covered me in my mother's womb.
¹⁴I will praise You, for I am fearfully *and* wonderfully made;
Marvelous are Your works,
And *that* my soul knows very well.
¹⁵My frame was not hidden from You,
When I was made in secret,
And skillfully wrought in the lowest parts of the earth.
¹⁶Your eyes saw my substance, being yet unformed.
And in Your book they all were written,
The days fashioned for me,
When *as yet there were* none of them.

Praise God for His precious thoughts about you.

[17]How precious also are Your thoughts to me, O God!
How great is the sum of them!
[18]*If* I should count them, they would be more in
number than the sand;
When I awake, I am still with You.

**Trust the Lord to deal with all your enemies,
whether men or spirits.**

[19]Oh, that You would slay the wicked, O God!
Depart from me, therefore, you bloodthirsty men.
[20]For they speak against You wickedly;
Your enemies take *Your name* in vain.
[21]Do I not hate them, O LORD, who hate You?
And do I not loathe those who rise up against You?
[22]I hate them with perfect hatred;
I count them my enemies.

**Allow the Lord to search your heart for any
unconfessed sin and to lead you in His truth.**

[23]Search me, O God, and know my heart;
Try me, and know my anxieties;
[24]And see if *there is any* wicked way in me,
And lead me in the way everlasting.

Psalm 140

*This psalm has elements of complaint and testimony, as
David brings some unspecified enemies before the Lord. Use
it to trust the Lord in the face of all adversity, whether tem-
poral or spiritual. Read 1 Peter 1:3–8.*

To the Chief Musician. A Psalm of David.

Consider the trials, temptations, or fears you may face this day. Trust the Lord to preserve you.

¹Deliver me, O Lord, from evil men;
Preserve me from violent men,
²Who plan evil things in *their* hearts;
They continually gather together *for* war.
³They sharpen their tongues like a serpent;
The poison of asps *is* under their lips.

Selah

⁴Keep me, O Lord, from the hands of the wicked;
Preserve me from violent men,
Who have purposed to make my steps stumble.
⁵The proud have hidden a snare for me, and cords;
They have spread a net by the wayside;
They have set traps for me.

Selah

Declare your confidence in the Lord and His salvation.

⁶I said to the Lord, "You *are* my God;
Hear the voice of my supplications, O Lord.
⁷O God the Lord, the strength of my salvation,
You have covered my head in the day of battle.
⁸Do not grant, O Lord, the desires of the wicked;
Do not further his *wicked* scheme,
Lest they be exalted.

Selah

Pray that God would deal with those—whether men or spirits—who would lead you astray or bring you to trial.

⁹"*As for* the head of those who surround me,
Let the evil of their lips cover them;

¹⁰Let burning coals fall upon them;
Let them be cast into the fire,
Into deep pits, that they rise not up again.
¹¹Let not a slanderer be established in the earth;
Let evil hunt the violent man to overthrow *him*."

Give thanks to God for His justice and care.

¹²I know that the LORD will maintain
The cause of the afflicted,
And justice for the poor.
¹³Surely the righteous shall give thanks to Your name;
The upright shall dwell in Your presence.

Psalm 141

In this psalm David is seeking the Lord's help for some very practical concerns. We can use it in the same ways, seeking God's wisdom and protection for our lives. Read Ephesians 5:15–18.

A Psalm of David.

Pray that God would protect you from sin in every area of your life.

¹LORD, I cry out to You;
Make haste to me!
Give ear to my voice when I cry out to You.
²Let my prayer be set before You *as* incense,
The lifting up of my hands *as* the evening sacrifice.

³Set a guard, O LORD, over my mouth;
Keep watch over the door of my lips.

[4]Do not incline my heart to any evil thing,
To practice wicked works
With men who work iniquity;
And do not let me eat of their delicacies.

Ask God to let you be open to correction from His servants.

[5]Let the righteous strike me;
It shall be a kindness.
And let him reprove me;
It shall be as excellent oil;
Let my head not refuse it.

Pray that God would deal with the wicked according to His justice and mercy.

For still my prayer *is* against the deeds of the wicked.
[6]Their judges are overthrown by the sides of the cliff,
And they hear my words, for they are sweet.
[7]Our bones are scattered at the mouth of the grave,
As when one plows and breaks up the earth.

Trust in the Lord to deliver you from temptations and trials.

[8]But my eyes *are* upon You, O GOD the Lord;
In You I take refuge;
Do not leave my soul destitute.
[9]Keep me from the snares *which* they have laid for
    me,
And from the traps of the workers of iniquity.
Let the wicked fall into their own nets,
While I escape safely.

Psalm 142

In this psalm of testimony David declares his confidence that the Lord will protect him in time of trouble. This psalm always reminds me of Paul and Silas praying and praising the Lord in the dungeon of that Philippian jail. Read Acts 16:16–25.

A Contemplation of David. A Prayer when he was in the cave.

Whatever your trial or fear, bring it to the Lord, who is our refuge.

¹I cry out to the Lord with my voice;
With my voice to the Lord I make my supplication.
²I pour out my complaint before Him;
I declare before Him my trouble.

³When my spirit was overwhelmed within me,
Then You knew my path.
In the way in which I walk
They have secretly set a snare for me.
⁴Look on *my* right hand and see,
For *there is* no one who acknowledges me;
Refuge has failed me;
No one cares for my soul.

Praise the Lord, and trust in Him to deal bountifully with you.

⁵I cried out to You, O Lord:
I said, "You *are* my refuge,
My portion in the land of the living.
⁶Attend to my cry,
For I am brought very low;
Deliver me from my persecutors,
For they are stronger than I.

⁷Bring my soul out of prison,
That I may praise Your name;
The righteous shall surround me,
For You shall deal bountifully with me."

Psalm 143

In this psalm of complaint David seeks deliverance, renewal, and guidance from the Lord. This is an excellent psalm to use when facing trials or seeking the Lord's will for some area of your life. Read 2 Thessalonians 3:1–5.

A Psalm of David.

Seek grace and mercy from the Lord in your time of need.

¹Hear my prayer, O LORD,
Give ear to my supplications!
In Your faithfulness answer me,
And in Your righteousness.
²Do not enter in judgment with Your servant,
For in Your sight no one living is righteous.

Remember the works of the Lord, and seek His strength in the midst of trials and temptations.

³For the enemy has persecuted my soul;
He has crushed my life to the ground;
He has made me dwell in darkness,
Like those who have long been dead.
⁴Therefore my spirit is overwhelmed within me;
My heart within me is distressed.
⁵I remember the days of old;
I meditate on all Your works;
I muse on the work of Your hands.

⁶I spread out my hands to You;
My soul *longs* for You like a thirsty land.

Selah

Seek guidance from the Lord for your trials and temptations.

⁷Answer me speedily, O LORD;
My spirit fails!
Do not hide Your face from me,
Lest I be like those who go down into the pit.
⁸Cause me to hear Your lovingkindness in the
    morning,
For in You do I trust;
Cause me to know the way in which I should walk,
For I lift up my soul to You.

⁹Deliver me, O LORD, from my enemies;
In You I take shelter.
¹⁰Teach me to do Your will,
For You *are* my God;
Your Spirit *is* good.
Lead me in the land of uprightness.

Seek grace for revival and deliverance from all foes.

¹¹Revive me, O LORD, for Your name's sake!
For Your righteousness' sake bring my soul out of
    trouble.
¹²In Your mercy cut off my enemies,
And destroy all those who afflict my soul;
For I *am* Your servant.

Psalm 144

David praises the Lord and testifies of his need of Him for deliverance and blessing. This is a good psalm to use in preparing for the day and interceding for children. Read Ephesians 6:1–9.

A Psalm of David.

Praise God, who cares for us though we are but a passing shadow.

¹Blessed *be* the LORD my Rock,
Who trains my hands for war,
And my fingers for battle—
²My lovingkindness and my fortress,
My high tower and my deliverer,
My shield and *the One* in whom I take refuge,
Who subdues my people under me.

³LORD, what *is* man, that You take knowledge of him?
Or the son of man, that You are mindful of him?
⁴Man is like a breath;
His days *are* like a passing shadow.

Trust the mighty God to deliver you from all trials and fears.

⁵Bow down Your heavens, O LORD, and come down;
Touch the mountains, and they shall smoke.
⁶Flash forth lightning and scatter them;
Shoot out Your arrows and destroy them.
⁷Stretch out Your hand from above;
Rescue me and deliver me out of great waters,
From the hand of foreigners,
⁸Whose mouth speaks vain words,
And whose right hand *is* a right hand of falsehood.

Praise God for the promise of deliverance.

⁹I will sing a new song to You, O God;
On a harp of ten strings I will sing praises to You,
¹⁰*The One* who gives salvation to kings,
Who delivers David His servant
From the deadly sword.

¹¹Rescue me and deliver me from the hand of
    foreigners,
Whose mouth speaks vain words,
And whose right hand *is* a right hand of falsehood—

Pray that God will bless the children of the church and all our homes and undertakings for Him.

¹²That our sons *may be* as plants grown up in their
    youth;
That our daughters *may be* as pillars,
Sculptured in palace style;
¹³*That* our barns *may be* full,
Supplying all kinds of produce;
That our sheep may bring forth thousands
And ten thousands in our fields;
¹⁴*That* our oxen *may be* well-laden;
That there be no breaking in or going out;
That there be no outcry in our streets.
¹⁵Happy *are* the people who are in such a state;
Happy *are* the people
whose God *is* the LORD!

Psalm 145

This is a psalm of glorious praise. Let it guide you to glorify the Lord for His goodness, mercy, and mighty works. Read Revelation 15:3–4.

A Praise of David.

Praise God for His majesty and His many mighty works.

¹I will extol You, My God, O King;
And I will bless Your name forever and ever.
²Every day I will bless You,
And I will praise Your name forever and ever.
³Great *is* the LORD, and greatly to be praised;
And His greatness *is* unsearchable.

⁴One generation shall praise Your works to another,
And shall declare Your mighty acts.
⁵I will meditate on the glorious splendor of Your
majesty,
And on Your wondrous works.
⁶*Men* shall speak of the might of Your awesome acts,
And I will declare Your greatness.
⁷They shall utter the memory of Your great goodness,
And shall sing of Your righteousness.

Praise God for His compassion and mercy.

⁸The LORD is gracious and full of compassion,
Slow to anger and great in mercy.
⁹The LORD is good to all,
And His tender mercies *are* over all His works.

Praise God for His glorious kingdom; pray that His people might declare His kingdom faithfully.

¹⁰All Your works shall praise You, O LORD,
And Your saints shall bless You.

[11]They shall speak of the glory of Your kingdom,
And talk of Your power,
[12]To make known to the sons of men His mighty acts,
And the glorious majesty of His kingdom.
[13]Your kingdom *is* an everlasting kingdom,
And Your dominion *endures* throughout all
    generations.

Praise God for His sovereign provision of all our needs.

[14]The LORD upholds all who fall,
And raises up all *those who are* bowed down.
[15]The eyes of all look expectantly to You,
And You give them their food in due season.
[16]You open Your hand
And satisfy the desire of every living thing.

Praise and bless the Lord, who hears and answers our prayers.

[17]The LORD *is* righteous in all His ways,
Gracious in all His works.
[18]The LORD *is* near to all who call upon Him,
To all who call upon Him in truth.
[19]He will fulfill the desire of those who fear Him;
He also will hear their cry and save them.
[20]The LORD preserves all who love Him,
But all the wicked He will destroy.
[21]My mouth shall speak the praise of the LORD,
And all flesh shall bless His holy name
Forever and ever.

Psalm 146

*Here is another psalm of praise that can lead us to glorify
the Lord for the many ways He helps and cares for us. Read
Philippians 4:10–20.*

Praise the Lord, and declare your trust in Him alone.

¹Praise the LORD!

Praise the LORD, O my soul!
²While I live I will praise the LORD;
I will sing praises to my God while I have my being.

³Do not put your trust in princes,
Nor in a son of man, in whom *there is* no help.
⁴His spirit departs, he returns to his earth;
In that very day his plans perish.

Praise the Lord for His power, truth, and gracious care.

⁵Happy *is he* who *has* the God of Jacob for his help,
Whose hope *is* in the LORD his God,
⁶Who made heaven and earth,
The sea, and all that *is* in them;
Who keeps truth forever,
⁷Who executes justice for the oppressed,
Who gives food to the hungry.
The LORD gives freedom to the prisoners.

⁸The LORD opens *the eyes of* the blind;
The LORD raises those who are bowed down;
The LORD loves the righteous.
⁹The LORD watches over the strangers;
He relieves the fatherless and widow;
But the way of the wicked He turns upside down.

Praise the eternal, sovereign God!

¹⁰The LORD shall reign forever—
Your God, O Zion, to all generations.

Praise the LORD!

Psalm 147

Use this psalm of praise to rejoice in the sovereign goodness of the Lord. Read 2 Peter 3:5–18.

Praise God for the many ways He is building His church.

¹Praise the LORD!
For *it is* good to sing praises to our God;
For *it is* pleasant, *and* praise is beautiful.

²The LORD builds up Jerusalem;
He gathers together the outcasts of Israel.
³He heals the broken-hearted
And binds up their wounds.
⁴He counts the number of the stars;
He calls them all by name.
⁵Great *is* our Lord, and mighty in power;
His understanding *is* infinite.
⁶The LORD lifts up the humble;
He casts the wicked down to the ground.

Praise the Lord for His care for creation.

⁷Sing to the LORD with thanksgiving;
Sing praises on the harp to our God,
⁸Who covers the heavens with clouds,

Who prepares rain for the earth,
Who makes grass to grow on the mountains.
⁹He gives to the beast its food
And to the young ravens that cry.

Pray that you might fear the Lord and hope more completely in Him.

¹⁰He does not delight in the strength of the horse;
He takes no pleasure in the legs of a man.
¹¹The LORD takes pleasure in those who fear Him,
In those who hope in His mercy.

Praise the Lord, who strengthens His church, its leaders, and its children, and meets all their needs.

¹²Praise the LORD, O Jerusalem!
Praise your God, O Zion!
¹³For He has strengthened the bars of your gates;
He has blessed your children within you.
¹⁴He makes peace *in* your borders,
And fills you with the finest wheat.

Praise God for His sovereign Word and for entrusting that Word to His people.

¹⁵He sends out His command *to the* earth;
His word runs very swiftly.
¹⁶He gives snow like wool;
He scatters the frost like ashes;
¹⁷He casts out His hail like morsels;
Who can stand before His cold?
¹⁸He sends out His word and melts them;
He causes His wind to blow, *and* the waters to flow.

¹⁹He declares His word to Jacob,
His statutes and His judgments to Israel.

[20]He has not dealt thus with any nation;
And *as for His* judgments, they have not known
them.

Praise the LORD!

Psalm 148

This glorious psalm of praise calls upon all creation to glorify Him. Use it in just that way in your own prayers. Read Revelation 4:1–11.

Call upon everything in the heavens to praise the Lord with you.

[1]Praise the LORD!

Praise the LORD from the heavens;
Praise Him in the heights!
[2]Praise Him, all His angels;
Praise Him, all His hosts!
[3]Praise Him, sun and moon;
Praise Him, all you stars of light!
[4]Praise Him, you heaven of heavens,
And you waters above the heavens!
[5]Let them praise the name of the LORD,
For He commanded and they were created.
[6]He has also established them forever and ever;
He has made a decree which shall not pass away.

Call upon everything in the earth to join you in praising the Lord.

[7]Praise the LORD from the earth,
You great sea creatures and all the depths;

⁸Fire and hail, snow and clouds;
Stormy wind, fulfilling His word;
⁹Mountains and all hills;
Fruitful trees and all cedars;
¹⁰Beasts and all cattle;
Creeping things and flying fowl;
¹¹Kings of the earth and all peoples;
Princes and all judges of the earth;
¹²Both young men and maidens,
Old men and children.

¹³Let them praise the name of the LORD,
For His name alone is exalted;
His glory *is* above the earth and heaven.
¹⁴And He has exalted the horn of His people,
The praise of all His saints—
Of the children of Israel,
A people near to Him.

Praise the LORD!

Psalm 149

Use this psalm of praise to pray that praise and rejoicing may increase among the people who know the Lord. Read 2 Corinthians 4:15.

Pray that praise might increase to God and that His people might know more of His salvation.

¹Praise the LORD!

Sing to the LORD a new song,
And His praise in the congregation of saints.

²Let Israel rejoice in their Maker;
Let the children of Zion be joyful in their King.
³Let them praise His name with the dance;
Let them sing praises to Him with the timbrel and
    harp.
⁴For the LORD takes pleasure in His people;
He will beautify the humble with salvation.

**Ask God to fill His people with joy and praise and
to send them forth to minister His Word to the
earth.**

⁵Let the saints be joyful in glory;
Let them sing aloud on their beds.
⁶*Let* the high praises of God *be* in their mouth,
And a two-edged sword in their hand,
⁷To execute vengeance on the nations,
And punishments on the peoples;
⁸To bind their kings with chains,
And their nobles with fetters of iron;
⁹To execute on them the written judgment—
This honor have all His saints.

Praise the LORD!

Psalm 150

The Book of Psalms concludes with a symphony of praise to the Lord and encourages us to make sweet music of praise to Him as well. Read Revelation 5:1–15.

Pray that God's creatures might praise Him greatly for His mighty acts.

> [1]Praise the Lord!
>
> Praise God in His sanctuary;
> Praise Him in His mighty firmament!
>
> [2]Praise Him for His mighty acts;
> Praise Him according to His excellent greatness!

Pray that praise to God might be full and glorious over all the earth.

> [3]Praise Him with the sound of the trumpet;
> Praise Him with the lute and harp!
> [4]Praise Him with the timbrel and dance;
> Praise Him with stringed instruments and flutes!
> [5]Praise Him with loud cymbals;
> Praise Him with high sounding cymbals!
>
> [6]Let everything that has breath praise the Lord.
>
> Praise the Lord!

A Seven-Week Schedule
for Praying the Psalms

This schedule is for praying through the Book of Psalms over a period of seven weeks. It suggests taking four periods during the day for praying the psalms: before your morning devotional reading (typically a portion of Psalm 119 or another psalm focused on the Word of God), then to guide your morning prayers, later at a time of your choice in midday, and finally before retiring at night.

Week One

	Sun	Mon	Tues	Wed	Thurs	Fri	Sat
Early Morning	119:1–8	119:9–16	119:17–24	119:25–32	119:33–40	119:41–48	119:49–56
Morning	16	8	5	93	100	136	30
Midday	46	72	27	80	13	56	40
Evening	138	4	113	143	41	123	149

Week Two

	Sun	Mon	Tues	Wed	Thurs	Fri	Sat
Early Morning	119:57–64	119:65–72	119:73–80	119:81–88	119:89–96	119:97–104	119:105–12
Morning	122	48	18	15	28	71	47
Midday	92	81	67	97	36	32	57
Evening	1	108	75	11	125	126	134

Week Three

	Sun	Mon	Tues	Wed	Thurs	Fri	Sat
Early Morning	119:113–20	119:121–28	119:129–36	119:137–44	119:145–52	119:153–60	119:161–68
Morning	50	43	66	49	68	127	38
Midday	14	144	79	82	87	17	64
Evening	3	110	115	133	128	22	103

Week Four

	Sun	Mon	Tues	Wed	Thurs	Fri	Sat
Early Morning	119:169–76	12	25	29	33	86	19
Morning	16	42	26	39	141	148	76
Midday	74	58	52	54	85	84	98
Evening	2	112	146	55	130	23	24

Week Five

	Sun	Mon	Tues	Wed	Thurs	Fri	Sat
Early Morning	119:1–8	119:9–16	119:17–24	119:25–32	119:33–40	119:41–48	119:49–56
Morning	111	44	51	73	101	107	37
Midday	96	117	121	131	129	89	34
Evening	9	145	60	59	147	65	62

Week Six

	Sun	Mon	Tues	Wed	Thurs	Fri	Sat
Early Morning	119:57–64	119:65–72	119:73–80	119:81–88	119:89–96	119:97–104	119:105–12
Morning	2	10	21	35	45	53	77
Midday	6	102	114	132	137	142	150
Evening	7	31	61	63	83	88	94

Week Seven

	Sun	Mon	Tues	Wed	Thurs	Fri	Sat
Early Morning	119:113–20	119:121–28	119:129–36	119:137–44	119:145–52	119:153–60	119:161–68
Morning	20	40	69	70	78:1–53	90	91
Midday	95	99	104	105	140	106	109
Evening	116	120	124	78:54–72	135	139	118

A One-Month Schedule for Praying the Psalms

This schedule is for praying through the Book of Psalms over a period of one month. It suggests three different periods of prayer during the day—morning devotions, midday, and evening. The morning period consists (in most cases) of three periods of prayer, which are an initial prayer of praise and thanksgiving, a portion of Psalm 119 or another psalm related to hearing God through His Word, which is to be used prior to Bible reading or study, and a psalm of intercession to guide your morning prayers. The midday period consists of various psalms of intercession, supplication, or complaint. The evening psalm is generally one of praise or resting in the Lord.

Week One

		Sun	Mon	Tues	Wed	Thurs	Fri	Sat
Morning	Praise and Thanksgiving	16	9, 59	8	96	108	113	147
	Hearing God through His Word	119:1–8	119:9–16	119:17–24	119:25–32	119:33–40	119:41–48	119:49–56
	Intercession	44, 122	27	90	7, 71	97	111	56, 70
Midday		80	46	116	21	107, 117	22	133
Evening		4	63	138	110	109	145	1

Week Two

		Sun	Mon	Tues	Wed	Thurs	Fri	Sat
Morning	Praise and Thanksgiving	121	146	148	92	47	48	136
	Hearing God through His Word	119:57–64	119:65–72	119:73–80	119:81–88	119:89–96	119:97–104	119:105–12
	Intercession	10, 45	115	88	132	57	73	129, 137
Midday		123	112	131	58, 130	61	69	43
Evening		3	149	91	134	75	86	28

Week Three

		Sun	Mon	Tues	Wed	Thurs	Fri	Sat
Morning	Praise and Thanksgiving	30	66	144	106	2	34	76
	Hearing God through His Word	119:113–20	119:121–28	119:129–36	119:137–44	119:145–52	119:153–60	119:161–68
	Intercession	50	17, 64	5, 18	124	83	94	72
Midday		11	20	13	15	120	23, 67	26
Evening		14	114	65, 150	24	6	62	87

Week Four

		Sun	Mon	Tues	Wed	Thurs	Fri	Sat
Morning	Praise and Thanksgiving	105	139	104	103	40	51, 89	85
	Hearing God through His Word	119:169–76	19	12	33	29	98	32
	Intercession	49, 84	60, 81	37	36, 38	35, 74	78	68
Midday		127	126	42	39	41	82	77
Evening		141	99	31	53	52, 55	93, 100	128

Week Five

		Sun	Mon
Morning	Praise and Thanksgiving	101	135
	Hearing God through His Word	143	95
	Intercession	118	140
Midday		79	102
Evening		54, 125	142

315

A One-Week Schedule for Praying the Psalms

This schedule is for praying through the Book of Psalms over a period of one week. It suggests seven periods of prayer, although the first two are generally kept together in practice, and the time you choose to pray can be flexible. I have made an effort to group psalms related to the passion of our Lord at the times of the week when the events suggested would actually have taken place, such as Psalm 22, the crucifixion psalm, which is set for Friday afternoon. Praying through the psalms weekly was a discipline commonly undertaken by church leaders throughout the ages, although it was recommended for all Christians. It may be especially useful during times of spiritual retreat or when seeking renewal in the Lord.

	Sun	Mon	Tues	Wed	Thurs	Fri	Sat
Rising	3, 9, 16, 111, 139	8, 45, 48, 112, 147	5, 18, 66, 99	15, 49, 93, 105	28, 68, 100, 104	29, 33, 71, 136	30, 47, 135, 142
Morning Devotions	119:1–24, 51, 73, 77, 95	119:25–48, 6, 19, 53, 72	119:49–72, 12, 67, 88, 114	119:73–96, 7, 26, 37, 101	119:97–120, 36, 39, 94, 148	119:121–44, 32, 102, 127, 141	119:145–76, 38, 57, 61, 86
Midmorning	2, 50, 78, 122	10, 43, 81, 144	27, 79, 83, 90	70, 80, 82, 97	13, 87, 106, 140	17, 56, 59, 62	40, 64, 98, 132
Noon	46, 92	21, 91	23, 117	121, 131	20, 24	85	25
Midafternoon	14, 74, 84, 118	58, 76, 96, 120	44, 52, 89, 129	35, 54, 60, 130	42, 116, 124	22, 31, 34, 69	65, 103, 137
Evening	1	108	75, 115	11, 133	125	107	128, 134
Retiring	63, 138	4, 110	113, 145	143, 146	41, 55, 109	123, 126	149, 150

Notes

Introduction

1. Abba Isaac, quoted in Owen Chadwick, ed., *Western Asceticism* (Philadelphia: The Westminster Press, 1958), 243–44.

2. Cf. Evan B. Howard, *Praying the Scriptures* (Downers Grove, Ill.: InterVarsity Press, 1999); Stanley L. Jaki, *Praying the Psalms: A Commentary* (Grand Rapids: William B. Eerdmans, 2001); Eugene H. Peterson, *Answering God: The Psalms as Tools for Prayer* (New York: HarperCollins, 1991); Ronald Quillo, *The Psalms: Prayers of Many Moods* (New York: Paulist Press, 1999).

3. Athanasius, *The Letter to Marcellinus*, trans. Robert C. Gregg (New York: Paulist Press, 1980), 110.

4. While there are numerous distinctly "Messianic" psalms—22, 69, and 110 come to mind—all the psalms, like the rest of Scripture, ultimately find their meaning in Jesus (John 5:39). As you pray through the psalms, you'll want to be careful to consider the work of Christ in all its aspects.

T. M. Moore is an associate pastor at Cedar Springs Church in Knoxville, Tennessee, and a former president of Chesapeake Theological Seminary in Baltimore. A prolific writer, he also serves as the North American editor for Scripture Union Publications. T. M. and his wife, Susie, have four children and ten grandchildren and make their home in Concord, Tennessee.